BOOGIE

SHMOOGIE

A Dispute Between Brothers

Gabriel Symonds

Copyright © Gabriel Symonds, Tokyo 2020

Second edition © Gabriel Symonds, Tokyo 2021

The Author asserts the moral right to be identified as the author of this work.

Published by Symonds Publications 2020

ISBN: 979-8-656635-59-2

All rights reserved. No part of this publication may be reproduced, stored in a retrieval system, or transmitted in any form or by any means, electronic, mechanical, photocopying, recording or otherwise, without the prior permission of the author.

This book is sold subject to the condition that it shall not, by way of trade or otherwise, be lent, resold, hired out or otherwise circulated without the author's prior consent in any form of binding or cover other than that in which it is published and without a similar condition including this condition being imposed on the subsequent purchaser.

BY THE SAME AUTHOR

Stop Smoking: Real Help at Last

Smoking is a Psychological Problem

Stop Smoking with the Symonds Method

Midlife: Problems and Solutions (Editor)

An English Doctor in Japan

Thou shalt not hate thy brother in thy heart.
Leviticus 19:17

And why beholdest thou the mote that is in thy brother's eye, but considerest not the beam that is in thy own eye?
Matthew 7:3

From envy, hatred, and malice, and from all uncharitableness, Good Lord deliver us.
The Book of Common Prayer

But is it not wonderful that a man...for whom his father did so much—that he should be stirred up by disappointed avarice to carry in his bosom for twenty years so bitter a feeling of rancour against those who are nearest to him by blood and ties of family!
Anthony Trollope, Orley Farm

Of all the vices which degrade the human character, Selfishness is the most odious and contemptible.
William Makepeace Thackeray, Vanity Fair

CONTENTS

	List of Illustrations	x
	Preface to the Second Edition	xi
	Introduction	xiii
1.	Family Background	1
2.	Tommy's Early Life	28
3.	Aches and Pains	35
4.	Girlfriends	44
5.	Problems	54
6.	Blaming Others	69
7.	The Death of John Symonds	81
8.	The Death of Renata Symonds	98
9.	Stolen Portrait and False Wills	113
10.	Challenging the Wills	121
11.	Neglected Grave	147
12.	Summary and Conclusion	168

LIST OF ILLUSTRATIONS

Following page 80

1. He would drive you potty
2. The *Dictionary* belongs to me
3. Bailiff Removal Notice
4. Return the £500 you stole from me
5. Where did all the money go?
6. Don't let him bully you
7. Cheque for £10,000
8. Joint account
9. Mother's message pad
10. Portrait receipt
11. Royal Society of Portrait Painters
12. Blackmail message
13. False claims
14. Brotherly love email
15. Cash gifts
16. Neglected grave
17. Unhappy and embittered

PREFACE TO THE SECOND EDITION

THE FIRST EDITION of this memoir attracted a number of criticisms and suggestions, some of which were made by people who were acquainted with my brother (Tommy) and me.

It was suggested that we should have considered using mediation to try to resolve the problems recounted in the book, such as with a trusted family friend, business partner, or perhaps a professional mediator. I would have welcomed this even though it would have been difficult because for over twenty years before the deaths of our parents I was (and still am) living in Japan. There was one person who seemed the obvious choice: the family accountant and apparent neutral family friend. I did appeal to this individual at the height of the difficulties towards the end of our parents' lives, but he allowed himself to be involved in a conflict of interest and was of no help at all. The only other possible person who might have been useful in this regard was a one-time colleague or friend of Tommy's called Theo Bradley. He offered his services as an intermediary when negotiations for a settlement were in trouble, but then disappeared from view.

It has also been pointed out that many of the incidents I relate over Tommy's extraordinarily intransigent behaviour are mirrored in complaints he makes against me in several emails which I quote in the book. Which came first? As readers might have difficulty judging the question, I should point out that these complaints are *projections*: he saw his own faults in me and accused me of behaviour that clearly came from him. As an example, there was the patently absurd idea that I 'bullied' our parents—something I had not the slightest wish or inclination to do.

Another criticism was: could I not have made the book more uplifting, particularly towards the end?

Unlike some other fraternal disputes where there is at least a modicum of willingness on both sides to compromise, what stands out in our case is my brother's utter intractability. In the end I was presented with an ultimatum: give in to his demands—or no deal. And he meant it.

I have tried to be fair and objective, and I hope that this revised edition will be improved by the incorporation of evidence in the form of a number of documents and photographs.

INTRODUCTION

ONE COULD NOT have wished for more decent or loving parents that John and Renata Symonds. They had two sons. I was the firstborn and Thomas Jeremy (Tommy) was eighteen months younger. Why have I written this account of Tommy's behaviour? The reasons are, first, to attempt to set the record straight by revealing the history of the treatment our parents suffered at his hands around the time of their deaths; and second, as a psychological study.

While I make no pretence of having behaved perfectly towards Tommy, I cannot recall any real slights or harms that I caused him which could even begin to justify his ill-will towards and resentment of me. Maybe he perceived me as being cleverer and more intelligent, or successful sooner than he, but if that is the case, envy is one of the most useless and destructive of human emotions; it did him no good and was positively harmful to us both.

Living on the other side of the world in Japan where I had immigrated to work as a doctor, there was little I could do at the critical times. On the other hand, Tommy lived within ten minutes' driving distance of our parents, and was a frequent—sometimes a daily or even twice daily—visitor, especially when in need of a meal. But it wasn't just physical nourishment he sought: he needed their constant support for all his problems. These were connected with business matters, girlfriend and other relationship difficulties, and very much to do with psychological and medical symptoms including those of an intimate nature. It seems he had a need, which our parents nearly always tried to satisfy, to *unburden* himself over such matters to a willing listener. Our mother in particular doubtless did what she thought was best, but being a professional psychotherapist she was probably not the ideal person to get so involved with him in this way: you cannot be objective about your own family!

It was not as if Tommy just needed a sympathetic ear or a shoulder to cry on from time to time. It went way beyond the normal support which children seek and parents readily give in times of trouble; it was *unending*. The repeated unburdenings, as well as the ready supply of sympathy and advice he sought and received, were of little help; they were never enough and he always wanted more. He would call mother nightly even in her old age to complain about all his problems. I witnessed this several times, as did a family friend. Worse still was a process of *grooming* of our parents by Tommy, carried out over something like ten years, with two aims: first, to obtain as much money as possible from their savings and eventually gain control of their bank accounts; and second, to disinherit me.

Especially when our parents were approaching the end of their lives, it should have been a time to set aside our differences (such as these might have been), and cooperate to try to ensure they were in as comfortable a situation as possible, consistent with their wishes. Unfortunately, as will be shown, Tommy's lack of cooperation with me extended to active obstructionism.

It seemed to me that our difficulties went far beyond the usual disagreements and jealousies that may occur between siblings. Tommy's extreme unreasonableness and rudeness to me, and even to our parents, to say nothing of his evident hatred of me, I think spilled over into pathology.

We could have been friends; that we were not is a matter of profound regret to me.

1

FAMILY BACKGROUND

TO UNDERSTAND THE problem of Tommy we need to start with our paternal grandparents.

The following narrative of our father's early life and relationships with his parents is taken from an account he sent me in February 1996 when he was aged 82. Into this I have incorporated some later addenda, together with a few comments in square brackets.

He begins with a quotation from C. G. Jung:

'Our souls as well as our bodies are composed of individual elements which were already present in the ranks of our ancestors.'[1]

I said that I would tell you in a letter something about my early life. What shall I put into the story and what shall I leave out as of insufficient importance? I do believe that I have been rather fortunate in my life, for, from a sad beginning, I slowly and painfully, but tenaciously and indomitably carved my own way towards an understanding of myself; and now in my old age I am able to write to you about myself, not in tragic circumstances as Oscar Wilde wrote from Reading Goal to Lord Alfred Douglas, but in circumstances of contentment. Although success in the world still eludes me, I have nothing to complain about and a lot to be grateful for, because I am in good health and at the height of my creative power.

I must quote these two sentences from Wilde's very long letter to Bosie Douglas: 'The fatal errors of life are not due to man's being unreasonable: an unreasonable moment may be one's finest moment. They are due to man's being logical.'

---

[1] C. G. Jung, *Memories, Dreams, Reflections*, Fontana Press, 1995, p 263.

About twenty-five years ago I realised that my ability could best be expressed in the writing of plays. 'What is a play?' asked the Spanish dramatist Lope de Vega, a contemporary of Shakespeare: 'Two boards and passion.' (The boards for the actors to strut and fret upon.)

If anyone should ask me which of my two parents influenced me the more, I should unhesitatingly reply, my mother. I would certainly not have been a dramatist and probably not an imaginative novelist were it not for that impossible woman.

On my father's side I came from a line of artists. My highly gifted and talented father, Robert Wemyss Symonds, was born on 31 December 1898. (Wemyss is a Scots name; there were Earls of Wemyss and March going back to the seventeenth century and there is the present Earl of Wemyss and March—see *Debrett's Peerage*.) He was the only child of William Robert Symonds and Margaret Symonds, née Swan, the sister of John Macallan Swan, a Scotsman who was a famous Victorian painter and sculptor; he died in 1910 and there is a detailed account of him in *The Dictionary of National Biography*.

My grandfather, William Robert Symonds, studied in Holland and Paris and earned a living as a portrait painter; he regularly exhibited at the Royal Academy. His portrait of Sir Richard Wallace is in the Wallace Collection, and his very fine pastel drawing of his son, Robert, dated 1911, hangs on the wall in my den.[2] Another sister of John Macallan Swan, Alice, who never married, was also an artist, trained by her brother. I own one of her watercolour paintings.

My father went as a day boy to St Paul's School, Hammersmith. He left that school at the age of 16, learnt shorthand and typing and worked as a secretary for a firm of antique dealers, but he didn't stay long in that job; he set himself up as an interior decorator and he bought and sold antiques at a good profit. Later he was made a Fellow of the Royal Institute of British Architects without taking a degree.

---

2 It now hangs on the wall in my apartment in Tokyo.

He was also made a Fellow of the Society of Antiquaries, a fellowship which is difficult to acquire. As well as being an historian of English furniture and clocks, he was an architect and one of his projects was the rebuilding of The Middlesex Hospital in 1928.

What sort of man was my father? He was a neurotic; there is no doubt about that. I showed his handwriting to a graphologist I knew, Hans Jacoby, who, after pondering on it for a moment or two, said: 'This is a very talented man, a wonderful judge of things, but a hopeless judge of people.' A perceptive remark! Did he understand himself; did he know what he was doing? No, he did not. In this connection Jung wrote: 'Our conscious intentions are continually disturbed and thwarted, to a greater or lesser degree, by unconscious intrusions whose causes are at first strange to us.'[3]

Now, into this cauldron was thrown an element that made the cauldron bubble—*my mother.*

> Double, double toil and trouble:
> Fire, burn; and, cauldron, bubble.
> (Macbeth)

Who was she, where did she spring from, and what was she like?

The country my mother came from was Lithuania, one of the Baltic states. Her maiden name was Luria. She was a woman of outstanding beauty with blue eyes and a flat Slav nose. I have a photograph of her as a young woman; her expression is thoughtful, even anxious. With her is her husband; she had been pushed into marriage at the age of 16 by her father, a well-to-do merchant. He was often in Germany. My mother knew that he had returned when she smelt the fumes of his cigar. He probably imported grain for the growing population of Germany.

---

[3] C. G. Jung, *The Archetypes and the Collective Unconscious*, Routledge & Kegan Paul, 1968, p 104.

Her husband, who was twice her age, was a photographer called Zapzels; she did not like him. They had a son called Chaim. This was a time when Jews emigrated from Eastern Europe to America, South Africa, Germany, Palestine, and other countries. Husband, wife, and baby came to England; then Mr Zapzels went on to South Africa to prepare the way for his young family who were being looked after in Manchester by a Polish-Jewish woman called Mrs Isaacs. It was the end of my mother's marriage.

My mother was totally illiterate, could neither read nor write. According to what she told me, her father thought it unnecessary for a woman to be literate; her husband would do all the reading and writing she needed. Of course, she might have had the urge to read and write in spite of what her father said, but she hadn't. She couldn't even read the time until my father taught her.

She had an elder brother but I don't know what he did.

Then Providence which rules our lives intervened. I have in my possession a silver cigarette case; it was given to her by my father and inscribed on the inside are the words: *In memory of 20-11-09* which, I take it, was the date my father and mother met.

It was a meeting by chance in a well-known café and restaurant by Piccadilly Circus on the north side, probably the Trocadero which was also a dance hall. On the front of the cigarette case is my father's crest, a unicorn with the words in a scroll underneath: VI ET ARTE (by strength and art).

When my father met my mother he was fascinated by her; she cast a spell over him. He was then 19. My father fell in love with her and she with him. He set her up in a flat in Battersea, furnished it and from time to time he would stay with her there but he did not live permanently with her. My father did everything for my mother except sanctify their relationship by marriage. On the envelope of his letters to her were the words 'Mrs Symonds' as the addressee. He furnished the flat in which my mother, my sister, and I lived with nice antique

4

things—engraved antique glasses, an eighteenth century carved sideboard with a marble top, etc., and the pastel portrait of himself, by his father, dated 1911, the year my sister was born; he paid for a nanny to look after us. My first photograph is of me in my pram, the nanny holding the pram handle, and my sister Eleanor beside the pram on her scooter.

My father's parents, conventional Victorians, must have been horrified at what their son and only child had done—taken up with this extraordinary Russian woman. Lithuania, like Poland, was then one of the western provinces of the Russian Empire.

My sister, Eleanor, was born in 1911 when my father was only 21, and I was born when he was 24. I was named John after my father's famous uncle, John Macallan Swan. My birth delighted him and he told my mother that he would send me to Eton—I am sure, at the time, he meant it. Furthermore, he signed the register of births and deaths (in Somerset House) under the name of Symonds; but my sister won't be found under the name of Symonds for she was registered under her mother's name. My father did not sign the register of her birth.

A nursemaid was employed from an agency in Belsize Lane, Hampstead (!)[4] to look after us. However, about the year 1915 or 1916, his ardour began to cool; it was the beginning of the end of their relationship. A year or two later my father broke away from my mother to her great distress; and he began to regard Eleanor and me as *her* children, nothing to do with him. But he continued to support her financially. Had he met another woman? I don't know but I think it probable. My mother was still in love with him but he was no longer in love with her.

Up till then his letters prove that he had been very much in love with her, saluting her as 'My darling Lil', and in one letter, 'My own darling Lil', and signing himself 'Bobbie', though

---

4 The exclamation mark (in the original) is because John and Renata Symonds lived in my flat at 81 Belsize Lane for the last twenty years of their lives.

more than once imploring her to stop making scenes.[5] But men easily fall in love—love at first sight—and just as easily fall out of love.

I am unaware of the precipitating factor which made my mother one day wait for him outside his office in Bruton Street, off Bond Street, and when he appeared, to attack him with her umbrella; but that is what she did. It then became a matter for lawyers—*his* lawyers, who wrote absurd letters to my mother. Here is part of one dated 10 July 2013:

> I am instructed that my client, Mr Robert Symonds, was seriously assaulted by Mrs Chappels[6] on Tuesday night. She forced herself into his Motor Car and somewhat seriously assaulted him, damaged his car, and created a considerable scene.
>
> This conduct, cannot of course, be tolerated. She moreover shouted to a man in the Street, that Mr Symonds was her husband and that she had discovered him in the company of another woman. My client is in real fear of Mrs Chappels' violence. I need hardly point out that, among other things, to molest a man in this way whilst driving a motor car might cause a very serious accident, and in fact, very nearly did so. Should my client have to suffer the least repetition of her conduct of last night he will be compelled to seek the usual protection.
>
> In view of Mrs Chappels' conduct and of the fact that she, a married woman, has ventured to commence an action against my client for Breach of Promise of marriage he is determined to have no more to do with her in the future than he is obliged. It is quite clear that Mrs Chappels has no legal claim upon him and on my instructions it is quite clear that she has no moral claim. All that Mr Symonds is willing to do is to pay her ten shillings a week for the maintenance

---

5 These letters were evidently sent in spite of her inability to read.
6 She called herself by the Anglicised form of Zapels, also spelt Sapzels.

of the child, being double the amount she could claim from him at the most under a successful Affiliation Summons, and this ten shillings per week he will only pay so long as he is satisfied she is properly caring for the child. Mr Symonds will if she prefers, instead of making her this allowance, gladly take charge of the child and provide for it.

Mrs Chappels has been up to now allowed to occupy the Flat at 38 Albert Mansions, Battersea, and to use the furniture in such Flat belonging to Mr Symonds, but in view of the above circumstances, I now, as Solicitor and Agent for Mr Symonds, determine any tenancy of permission, which has entitled her to occupy the Flat and to use the furniture, and call upon her to vacate such Flat, and to deliver over vacant possession thereof, together with the furniture therein to him. Mr Symonds has no desire that Mrs Chappels shall be unreasonably inconvenienced and he will, therefore, give her till the end of next week to vacate the Flat and hand over the furniture, but, if she does not deliver over the Flat and furniture to him during next week, he will take immediate proceedings, without further notice for their recovery.

What a low lot solicitors are! In one letter they demanded to know when their client had promised to marry her. He had undoubtedly promised to marry her; he had promised her the earth as long she continued to love him. A covenant was drawn up: he would pay her £200 a year, £3 a week, as long as she left him in peace. The average working wage then was £2 a week or less.

[As shown by extracts from bills sent by Mrs Chappels' lawyer[7], the matter didn't end there.]

In 1914 an 'Indenture' (drawn up by some stupid lawyers) between my father and mother for the purpose of settling the

---

[7] She was at that time assisted by a barrister friend, Mr Abinger, who was in Margate where John with his mother and sister later went to live.

dispute: he agreed to pay her £150 per annum, and to let her keep the furniture he'd given her. One would think that this was the end of the matter, but not at all, for on 6 January 1916 a new Indenture as drawn up:

> LILLIE SAPZELS on the one part…and ROBERT SYMONDS on the other part SUPPLEMENTAL to an Indenture dated the eighth of June 2014… has broken her covenant not to molest or interfere with the said Robert Symonds and in consequence he has suffered financial harm and his business has been damaged and he has therefore refused to continue the payments provided for in the Principal Deed and WHEREAS the said Lillie Sapzels has requested the said Robert Symonds to make some provision for the two children mentioned in the Principal Deed which he has agreed to NOW THIS INDENTURE WITNESSETH as follows: [Nine separate clauses follow]

Meanwhile my sister and I continued to live at the flat in Battersea as if nothing at all had changed.

It is clear, however, that my mother's 'happiness' with her lover, 'Bobbie', ceased before I was born; then their relationship started up again, and the same love-hate pattern continued until RWS could stand it no more.

My mother packed up everything and moved to Cliftonville, a suburb of Margate. My mother went there because Mrs Isaacs, who was a mother figure to her, had gone there from Manchester. For £25 a year we rented a three-storied house. So there in quiet Cliftonville my mother, sister, and I lived; we could afford to go as day children to small private schools, for the fees were only 2 guineas a term. From our rich father in London we never received any Christmas or birthday presents; as far as he was concerned we didn't exist. It was absurd.

Then a bombshell exploded in his life; it was entirely unexpected. My father knew that it would do far more harm to his business activities than my mother did by waiting for him in the street and when he appeared attacking him, or might do in the future.

The year when this happened, I think, was 1920. How did it come about? He had fallen in love with a Mrs Thelma Bamberger and wanted to marry her—not my poor mother whom he had ditched—but Mrs Bamberger and she wanted to marry him. Unfortunately she was married to Mr Bamberger. Did RWS think it was time he took the plunge and got married? So Mrs B instituted divorce proceedings by inventing (with Mr B's connivance?) a neat and foolproof story of adultery. But this scheme was knocked on the head by the King's Proctor—the King being George V—and Mrs B to her surprise and my father's alarm, found herself in the dock at the Old Bailey on the charge of perjury, of naughtily telling lies to get a divorce. My father's photograph was in the popular papers and my mother and her two children mentioned.

I recall that Mrs B paid us a visit in Margate. Would my mother help her?[8] (Had RWS and Mrs B fallen out?) My mother ran to that brilliant barrister, Mr Abinger who had befriended her, and he told her what was obvious: to keep out of it.

My father, alarmed, threw my mother a *douceur*: he would pay the fees for Eleanor and me to go to a very nice private boarding school called St Stephen's in Folkestone, run by two Victorian sisters, thereby giving my mother a rest. He must have found that school which took boys till the age of 9 (I was then 7) and girls until they went to the university. At table, the girls were not allowed to speak unless they spoke in French. We were there for a year, a happy one for Eleanor and me.

Meanwhile the great Bamberger trail dragged on and concluded with Mrs B being sent to prison for nine months. Absurd.

Then RWS behaved typically: the trial was over, the danger had passed and he decided that he could not longer afford

---

8 Presumably by renouncing her claims on RWS.

to pay for us to stay on at St Stephen's! So we had to leave. Needless to say he was earning a great deal of money at the time.

(During the mid-30s after I had returned from Spain [see below], I read in the *Evening Standard* that Mrs B had been up to some naughty business, was again at the Old Bailey, found guilty and sentenced to four years' imprisonment. I said cheerfully to my father when I entered his office with the newspaper in my hand, 'Your old girlfriend is in trouble again!' It was a remark that he failed to find funny.)

Society in England during my early years was vastly different from what it is today. To be born out of wedlock was considered a disgrace; today it frequently happens and no one bothers about it. Natural children (as they used to be called) now have exactly the same rights as those born after their parents' marriage.

It was a friend of my sister's, a man who had qualified in medicine at Guy's Hospital, who suggested to her and to me that we were illegitimate; I was then 15. I felt he was right and had supplied me with a missing piece of the jigsaw puzzle. I didn't discuss the matter with my mother—I suppose I didn't want to embarrass her.

The most humiliating incident in my young life was in 1924 when I was 10. I was at a school called Cliftonville College, a private boarding and day school. One day the headmaster stopped me in the road as I was on my way home for lunch and said to me, 'Can't your mother buy you a new suit?' I then grew aware that I was wearing a shabby suit such as only very poor children might wear. I ran home angry and confused. What happened? My mother and I set out together. She had realised that she had to buy me a new suit but she, being incredibly mean, did not want to pay much for it. It was easier to get blood out of a stone than to get her to part with money. We stopped outside a shop that sold suits for boys; they were hung on a pole outside the shop, the cheapest suits ever. An argument broke out between us. I can't remember what happened after that.

Needless to say I never had any toys. I remember trying to persuade my mother to part with *one penny* of the old currency to buy me a jigsaw puzzle at a jumble sale. I succeeded with difficulty.

Someone gave Eleanor a very nice doll; it had a porcelain face and opened and shut its eyes. My mother took it away from Eleanor. 'This is too good a doll for you to play with every day; you can have it only on Sundays.' It is not surprising that Eleanor never had any children.

I needn't tell you about other incidents that reveal her extraordinary meanness, ignorance, arrogance, and utter stupidity. It wasn't as if she was poor. We lived in lower middle-class circumstances. She was stupid for having gone to live in Margate; she should have stayed in Battersea and appealed to my father for anything extra we needed. It would have been easier had she been living in the same town; he was only across the water in Chelsea. In those days he was earning so much money that I am sure he would have coughed up without an argument.

Much later (it was about 1951) when I was independent and had my own family, I visited him at his flat at Shelley Court, Tite Street, Chelsea. As he and I were entering the dining room, he said, 'Things today are not as they were in the twenties when I was earning £40,000 a year.' In the twenties, with low income tax, that was a very large income. 'Were you really?' I replied to him. 'Well, it was a pity that you didn't send a little money down Margate way.' My remark spoilt his dinner, but not mine. In the twenties he rented a house in Cheyne Row, the house had a porch, and he was the owner of a Rolls Royce and employed a chauffer.

I do not recall any of these things with bitterness, for I overcame them all and grew stronger because of them. Nietzsche, who was a very great psychologist, said: *If the poison doesn't kill you, it will make you stronger.* I made my way in the world not in spite of these things but *because* of them.

I'll add one incident from my childhood which encapsulates the whole situation: on one Christmas Eve the postman delivered to us a parcel. My sister and I eagerly tore the wrapping off. A moment later there was a loud knocking at the door. The postman again; the parcel wasn't for us at all, but for the people next door!

From an early age—could I have been 5?—I found my mother's behaviour embarrassing. I was ashamed of her. She looked English; her features were refined but her behaviour was far from English behaviour.

Her attitude to me was extraordinary. She loved me passionately; there is no doubt about that. She told me that were it not for me she would have committed suicide at the break-up of her relationship with my father. But her love for me was of the most deadly kind. I found a friend, an older boy who lived in the next street; he was an apprentice of a watch and clock mender. He took me on the back of his bicycle to the Birchington Marshes where I saw from the top of the hill a heron flying over the dykes. We descended, entered a wood, and I saw other marvellous sights—a rookery, woodpeckers, etc. My mother hated this friendship of mine and she accused this boy to his face of stealing an ornate sliver whistle, a child's toy, which she had mislaid. What she meant, without realising it, was that he was stealing *me* from her. I was not allowed to have any friends. She had lost the man she loved and I had taken his place.

But you can't stop children in a small community from making friends. My best friend was Alan Weston, the son of a well-to-do dairyman who supplied milk, etc., to the people in the Isle of Thanet. He would call on me and tinkle his bicycle bell in the road; this sent a signal to me. My mother said to me, 'If he continues to call on you, I shall complain to his father.' I told Alan and he replied, 'Oh, my father knows how to deal with customers like your mother.'

Shortly afterwards, Alan decided to call on me again. Cliftonville in those days was a very quiet little own in the residential area; there were no aeroplanes flying overhead, no TV, no cars, no wireless sets. A greengrocer came to our street in a van which was pulled by a horse.

Now, at the very hour that Alan was coming to call on me in defiance of my mother, he was by chance preceded by another boy called, I think, Chambers (Christian name forgotten) who wanted to be my friend. He was a delicate boy, so much so that he didn't go to school but was taught at home by a tutor. When my mother heard his gentle tapping on the door, she thought that this was Alan and that he had come to take me away from her (as another woman had taken my father away from her). She sprang up in a fury—we were having lunch together—seized a broom to demolish him with and screaming like a madwoman, tore up the passage. She flung open the door to find a complete stranger. What she said to him I don't know or I've long forgotten. Poor Chambers almost had a heart attack. As for Alan several streets away, he heard those mad screams, put on the brake of his bicycle and dismounted in a state of unbelief and amazement. A day later he said to me, 'I didn't know that your mother was like *that*. I shall never call on you again.' And he never did. My description of this incident is in no way an exaggeration.

When I was 15 Alan Weston asked me—we were riding our bicycles up the street at the time—what I was going to do when I left school. I replied with these words: 'I am going to be a writer.' I remember the incident because he was astonished. I did not know why I had said that, but future events cast a shadow. Three years later when I was ill with the flu in Madrid, an English friend brought to my bedside a book of short stories which he had borrowed from the Anglo-American library in the city. Among the stories was Robert Louis Stevenson's *A Lodging for the Night*, about Francois Villon; this moved me so much that in one remarkable moment I knew consciously that I wanted to be a writer. It was the beginning, the first step, towards my becoming a dramatist.

At the end of the spring term 1930, having reached the age of 16, I left school. The school I was then at was called Stanley House School which was modelled on public school lines; previously I'd been at a school called Devon House School. I had left Cliftonville College because that school had moved to Ramsgate. The master of Stanley House asked me what I was going to do in life, to which I replied, 'I am going to do nothing, nothing at all.' He snorted and said, 'As I would expect from you!' The boys at that school if they were lucky and had taken successfully matriculation would get jobs as bank clerks or as clerks in estate offices. It was two years later that I realised, consciously, that I wanted to be a writer, so what I meant by 'nothing' was that I was waiting until something occurred to me. I had no advice from my mother and I'd not met my father.

There was nothing for me to do in Margate, so in the summer of 1930 I decided to set out in search of my father; I felt that there was a future for me in him. So I went by train to London and made my way to his office at 7 Bruton Street. I was a timid youth, uncertain of myself; I was *lost*. I rang the bell at the street door on which was a brass plate bearing the legend SYMONDS AND LUTYENS. It was not Sir Edwin Lutyens[9] the famous architect but his son Robert[10] who was also an architect, and not a very good one. Many years later I asked my father why he was in partnership with Robert Lutyens; he replied, 'Because he knew a lot of rich people,' i.e., he brought in commissions. Under my father were seven qualified architects.

---

9 The widow of Sir Edwin—Sir Edwin had designed all the principal buildings in New Delhi—had, through the Indian influence, become a Theosophist and when John Symonds's biography of Madam Blavatsky, *The Lady with the Magic Eyes*, was published in 1959 she wrote him an appreciative letter; it was Blavatsky's Theosophical Society that Lady Lutyens was drawn into.

10 John Symonds wrote to me (Gabriel Symonds) that during the late 1940s he had met Robert Lutyens again in the Berkeley grill room: Lutyens had fallen on his feet for he had married a very rich Jewish woman from New York.

I rang the bell, then rang it again. Someone came down and said, 'You don't ring the bell, you just walk up.' The offices were on the upper floors. I asked for Mr Symonds; he was out, but was expected back soon. I declined to say what I wanted to see Mr Symonds about. On the first floor was the main office in the front overlooking the street and, facing the back, an anteroom. So there I apprehensively waited, my school cap in my hand. My father appeared; he looked at me and I looked at him. I didn't have to ask him who he was, neither did he ask me who I was: he knew, he knew, *he knew!* He said nothing. I said, 'There are people waiting for you in there.' There were. So he went in to see them. This shows how timid I was and how I was more concerned about other people that I was about myself. With a quickly beating heart I waited for him to reappear. After some time he did so and said quietly, 'Go back to your mother.' Well, thank you very much! So without a word I left, glad to get away from the place and make my way back to Margate.

I had left school and met my father. What was the next step? There was nothing I wanted to do or could do in Margate, so I told my mother that we must move to London. Through an estate agent we saw a badly converted flat on the first floor of an old building set in its own grounds at 77 Clarence Road, Clapham. 'This will do,' I said straight away, without seeing other places or even carefully considering this one. So we left Margate and with all our furniture came in the year 1930 to Clapham.

Next, Providence directed my footsteps towards the reading room of the British Museum, the room with its high dome in which Karl Marx had written his inflammatory books. I do not know why I went there; no one had told me to, so that is why I ascribe it to Providence. The clerk who dealt with applicants in a room outside the reading room said after a careful look, 'But you are not 21.' No one was permitted to enter the reading room under that age. I stoutly averred that I was. (I'd hidden my school cap.) He didn't pursue the matter, and so, while still aged 16, the doors of the reading room opened to me. It was a momentous event in my life, something unimaginable to my school companions. What books should I read there? I began with books about wild birds; then I soon moved on to philosophy and French authors in translation. Balzac, because of his prodigious labours at novel writing, became my hero.

At this time, the spring of 1931, I was hoping to make contact again with my father; but this time I wasn't going to approach him. That task was left to my mother; to assist her she asked an elderly Margate solicitor called Weigall who had a soft spot for her. He was an eighteenth century character rather like Dr Johnson. He went to London to ask my father what, if anything, he would do for me. He called by appointment at 7 Bruton Street. I was not privy to their conversation so I don't know how it went. I only know that Mr Weigall was tremendously impressed by Mr Robert Symonds of Symonds and Lutyens, architects, to my disgust. Nonetheless, the upshot was that my father agreed to meet me. But do not think that he had seen the light and was prepared to be reasonable and treat me in a fair-minded way. Not a bit of it.

Our relationship got off to a slow start. He did not regard me as his son although he had no other son, only two stupid and grasping daughters. I was a kind of phantom that haunted him and from which he couldn't escape. I remember sitting with him in a taxi; we were going to have lunch together in a restaurant in Holborn. He asked me what I would like to do in life. I replied that I should like to study old English furniture; my choice of that subject was owing to my identification with him. He suggested that I study old paintings instead. This was before I realised a year later that fate had decided that I was to be a writer. How was I to live? He was still paying £200 a year to my mother; he knew that if he stopped that, she would kick up a fantastic fuss. So, he proposed that I read the seventeenth and eighteenth century newspapers in the British Museum library for information about joiners, cabinet-makers, and clock-makers. He would pay my expense—fares, lunch, etc. I itemised everything: my expenses came to less than £1 a week. When they went up a little, he complained that I was getting extravagant; he was not made of money! But he did not know how long I spent researching for him in the newspaper library and how long I spent at my own studies in the main reading-room: an hour's work for him, six or seven hours for myself! I called frequently at 7 Bruton Street with what I had found for him in the newspaper library, copied out by hand, then typed.

I had not known how to type but he paid for me to learn at Pitman's in Southampton Row. Also, from time to time he gave me one of his Saville Row suits that he'd got tired of; they fitted me well. But in spite of our developing relationship I was never invited to his house in Cheyne Row, Chelsea.

Now I come to the mysterious heart of the matter. Instead of being grateful to my father I quarrelled with him and he could do nothing about it. Was he afraid of me? No. The situation had caught him, he couldn't get away from it, and he didn't want to.

You would think that our relationship had at last been established on a more or less reasonable basis. Not a bit of it. What had been established between him and me was a relationship which took on nightmarish proportions. It is beyond my ability to describe the struggles that would go on weekly between my father and me. As he didn't want his staff of qualified architects who were working on the top floor to hear us, he took me out of the ante-room on the first floor to trade insults on the stairs that led to the street door. The staff knew of course what was going on; they weren't stupid, besides I looked like him especially as I wore his cast off suits. More than once when we were having a row, he threatened to call the police; I defied him to do so.

I am referring to the first year or so of our bizarre relationship. The reason for this was that RWS didn't know what he was doing—and I'm not sure that I knew what I was doing—and he didn't understand himself; he lived from his consciousness which said one thing, his unconsciousness another; he was devoid of moral feeling and he was a bully. I would say that he was struggling with an unconscious force which held him it its grip, and which he projected onto me. The tension and hatred on either side was considerable. But he was always drawn back to me and once said to me, in despair, 'You used to plague my life with communism; now it's psychology,' a remark that I recall with a smile.

I, for my part, hadn't the strength to tell him to go to hell and then I would disappear into the London fog, never to return to 7 Bruton Street. I wanted what I had never had—a father. He was trying to get away from his past which I represented. When he had occasion to write to me, he addressed me as 'Dear John' and signed himself, not even as 'Robert' but 'RWS'. He was totally unconcerned about my future.

Another incident: he informed me that he was someone important in the world; and what was I? Nothing and nobody. I thought at the time that his boasting about himself was absurd, for in those days I hadn't begun my real career and I never felt hurt at all at his denigration of me. What he meant, without knowing it, was that he, consciously, was an important chap, and anything in his unconscious—me—that contradicted it wasn't real, was nothing! I do recall saying to him, 'Oh, shut up, Robert. You will be remembered only because of me!'

He wasn't aware of it but he *needed* to quarrel with me: go back to the quotation from Jung about our conscious intentions being continually disturbed and thwarted by unconscious intrusions. I have a letter in which he wrote to my mother—it is undated but it was either 1930 or 1931: 'Will you inform your son that I will not put up with his conduct. I have tried to be nice to him and to help him and the only thanks I receive in return is for him to worry me at my office by constantly telephoning and coming round and writing me an impertinent letter. When I first met him he made upon me a favourable impression but his recent behaviour is such that I shall have nothing more to do with him unless he can behave in a proper manner and treat people older than himself with respect.'

He could easily have stopped my visits to him and the rows we had on the stairs of 7 Bruton Street had he wanted to, but as I've said he needed those nightmarish situations. I, for my part, got fed up with them and I informed him that I wanted to go to live in Spain. This was in 1932 when I was 18. Here is a quotation from the letter he wrote to me:

> Dear John, I have received your letter and I have nothing further to say concerning your wish to go to Spain. I cannot in these times agree to send you £1 a week for an indefinite period and I also know that you could never stand the hardships that you would experience in living in a country like Spain on so small a sum. With regard to my meeting you I will do so if you control yourself and talk sensibly about your future. I will not, however, listen to the raving of a young man whose temper gets the better of him because he is unable to get his own way in everything...

[It appears at this stage that John temporarily ceased working for his father although contact with him was maintained.]

I found myself a job with a picture restorer in Piccadilly; he agreed to take me on as a kind of apprentice, to teach me how to restore old masters. For the first two years he would pay me nothing, then £1 a week during the third year, £2 a week during the next year, and so on. My father agreed to continue to pay me 'expenses' while I was being trained by this picture restorer. At the end of the discussion with him—it took place in our flat in Clapham, my mother being present—RWS said regretfully, 'I suppose I shan't see you any more.' He didn't want me to disappear.

After a few weeks I got the sack from the picture restorer. I was not really employable in any capacity. His last words to me before I went down the stairs with a feeling of relief were, 'You will get on in the world all right because you have the gift of the gab.'

I didn't want to return to 7 Bruton Street. I decided to go to Spain and told RWS so. For a reason that I can't understand he agreed after all to let me go there and to send me monthly a small amount of money which enabled me to live cheaply in Madrid for four months over the winter of 1932–33. He gave me £15 for the fare to Madrid and sent me £1 a week. In Madrid I found in an old part of the town a lodging house which charged me 2 shillings and 3 pence a day for bed and board. My father missed me and on the excuse that he couldn't afford to send me £1 a week any longer begged me to come home.

And in Madrid as I've said the realisation came to me that Providence had decided that I was to be a writer. However, it was not until 1940 that I had a short story published and then a poem.

On my return to London I recontinued my work for RWS.

[The next recorded event in this history deals with the death of John's mother.]

On 12 December 1955 my mother telephoned me; she was feeling unwell, she said. Would I call on her? Yes, of course. I had no key to the street door but I was let in by her landlady, Mrs Flicker, who was going out when I arrived. I went upstairs to my mother's flat on the first floor: the sitting-room door was open, the electric fire was on, but where was my mother? She wasn't in her kitchen. (Her sitting room in the front was also her bedroom.) I grew aware of an eerie silence. Something was wrong. I apprehensively opened the lavatory door which wasn't locked. My mother was lying, slumped on the floor, beside the lavatory bowl. I knew that she was dead. I was shocked and terribly upset. There wasn't a telephone in her flat. I ran out of the house and across the road, knocked on the nearest door and begged to use the telephone which was in the hall—it was a telephone into which one fed coins. I knew the number of my mother's doctor. I spoke to the telephone operator, asking her to ring the doctor; she did, and came back to me to say that the doctor's phone was engaged. 'Break into the conversation; it is urgent,' I said. She did so and I spoke to the doctor. She said he would come immediately. And she did. Together we carried my poor mother to her bed. Her face had a grim expression and was ashen grey. I'd never seen a dead body before. This was her journey's end; she was about 70.

As she was alone at the time of her death, the coroner ordered an autopsy. I transcribed the cause of her death: 'Ruptured aneurysm of thoracic descending aorta; hypertension.' On one occasion I had witnessed a terrific and frightening nose bleed which had required a whole towel to absorb.

[I interpose here a brief account, taken from another of John's letters to me, of what became of Chaim. He also gives more detail about Mr Abinger who helped Lillie in her trouble with RWS.]

Now, who was Mr Abinger? In the first place his name wasn't Abinger but Abrahams, a Jewish name. He was a brilliant barrister. For hundreds of years Jews strove to get away from Jewry, and married non-Jews.

Mr Abinger was married to a woman who'd been a hospital nurse. They had a fine house in Cliftonville, Margate, which house they turned into a zoo. I recall visiting them. In very large cages were many exotic birds of brilliant colours. They also kept monkeys. Chaim went to live with them. I have (or had) a photograph of Mr Abinger standing on the steps of his house in the sun, Mrs Abinger lower down with a monkey in her arms and Chaim on the pavement. As they had no children they more or less adopted Chaim who wasn't happy living with his mother in her distraught state. Mr Abinger wanted to bring him into his legal practice so that he would in time become a lawyer, but Chaim was without ambition or brains and joined the British Army (for seven years) instead. It was unlike the British Army of today which is difficult to get into; you have to be pretty clever. For Chaim to have become a private in the British Army of those days was a mark of his failure.

When he was grown my mother once called on her son Chaim. He wasn't at home but his frightfully ugly and vulgar wife, Rose, was, and my mother lambasted her for their not loving her. The consequence of that visit was that Chaim never wanted to see her again and he and Rose slunk off to Canada without saying goodbye; they had emigrated.

[From several others of John's letters to me I have compiled this further history of his mother.]

Her life had brought her a little happiness which was reflected in the many loving letters my father wrote to her; then when he left her she grew bitter and demanding, even mad at times. She was not, however, in poverty for the money my father paid her and continued to pay her until I telephoned to tell him that she was no more, enabled her to live in lower middle-class circumstances; she never earned a penny or tried to. I also used to give my mother a little money when I had it to spare, but it wasn't enough for her to realise her wishes and fantasies.

Could her life have been different? When I was a child I tried to teach her to read; and I tried again during the 1940s; it was hopeless. Her mind wasn't on it. What she failed to do in that respect I did for her because I became an author.

She would listen to the wireless and play patience. She did not accept her fate and make the best of it. She had no religion or philosophy of life.

I can't say her life was wasted because she had three children; I was the one she loved the most. What had my mother done? She'd slipped loose from her husband whom she couldn't stand and from her background which she didn't like. In 1908 or 1909 she left Panevezys in Lithuania and travelled by train and boat to England, and went with her little son Chaim to stay with Mrs Isaacs in Manchester.

My mother then went to London and by chance met my father. For a time it must have seemed as if he would fulfil her wildest dreams. But all happiness is only temporary. My parents were very different from each other—in their background, behaviour, and outlook.

Would her life have been better had she followed her husband to South Africa? Impossible to say. She despised him and loved my father. Her life was otherwise empty. This made her quarrelsome.

When I was living independently with my own family she would call on me frequently and would always ask if I had any news. One day I was able to tell her some news. I told her in these precise words: 'She is dead and you are alive.' My mother knew what that meant. My father's then wife, Daphne, had killed herself, and was therefore dead. I have called my father a neurotic; it is not an exaggeration. It was no fun being married to him. My mother, poor woman, exclaimed when I told her more, 'He'll marry me yet!'

With Daphne out of the way my mother took to telephoning RWS and, I believe, meeting him. So far so good. But one day shortly afterwards RWS told me he was going to marry a woman called Monica. I said to him, 'That's your business but don't for God's sake tell my mother.'

Monica was an upper-class woman, the daughter of Sir H. M. Grayson, Bt. She was uneducated, a talebearer, and troublemaker. If she had no trouble to report to RWS she invented it. She caused trouble between RWS and Virginia (the daughter of RWS and Daphne) and between him and me by her talebearing.

Now, my father had a housekeeper in his flat at Shelley Court, Tite Street, and one day when RWS and Monica were in Suffolk together, my mother telephoned and the housekeeper answered. The stupid woman said to my mother, 'Is that Mrs Symonds?' 'What?! Has he married again?' 'Yes, don't you know?'

My mother came tearfully to me and I, fed up with this impossible situation said, 'Oh, for God's sake, can't he have a little happiness in his old age?!'

RWS and Monica returned to Shelley Court and I called there during the evening to find my father in a rage and Monica drunk and in her nightie; he had flung the front door open and was ordering her to get out. Get out where? Into the street, I suppose. 'Oh, for God's sake, Robert,' I said, 'I told my mother who had found out that you had married again, that you were entitled to a little happiness in your old age.' I think this brought RWS to his senses and enabled Monica, who was weeping, to sneak back to bed.

[The death of John's father is related in a letter dated 15 September 1958 that he wrote to his friend Jacques Calmy.]

A week ago my father died at the age of 68. It was reported at some length in *The Times* and *The Daily Telegraph*, his achievements and character extolled. I could have written a more detailed account of his character. I did not go to his funeral because I am not a hypocrite and anyhow it took place in the churchyard next door to his country estate. He left quite a bit of money but not, alas, to me. The absurd thing is that he spent more time with me than with anyone else, I wrote his best books for him, and in spite of a final break and bitter words we had not a little amount of affection for each other. When I took up with him again after the war, and begun the more serious task of educating him, a shadow was thrown over our relationship because of his fear that through my own writing I (his dark secret) should get known . Now it is all over.

***

This account, which I re-read in 2020, does much to explain why our father treated my brother and me in the way he did. It is hard to believe that, at the time, he 'never felt hurt at all' by

RWS's denigration of him. Being brought up by an illiterate single parent—a mother whom he describes as arrogant, mean, paranoid, and at times insane—and having no contact with his own father till the age of 16, is more than enough to explain his timidity. It also explains why, as he told me, that when he applied to join the Royal Air Force during the Second World War, although there was a desperate need for pilots, he was turned down on the grounds that he was too neurotic. He thus at times floundered in trying to bring up his own sons. Sometimes he would even tell me, 'I never had a father, and I didn't know how to bring up children.' This infuriated me because I could not understand how, as a grown man and someone who was vastly more experienced that I, a mere child, he could say this to justify the difficulties he found in being a father himself. At such times I indeed wondered who was the parent and who the child.

The stingy atmosphere in which father grew up with his mother seemed to have produced the opposite characteristic when he became adult: he was ever over-generous. Although for a while after the Second World War, like so many people we lived hand-to-mouth, from time to time he would receive a windfall of an advance on royalties for his books, but would immediately spend it, usually on his family, and until late in life had no idea of saving.

***

I also need to give some account of our mother's background, but I unfortunately I know little about it. This is because, for reasons that will be clear from what follows, she hardly ever spoke of her early life.

Renata Symonds, née Israel, was born on 7 August 1913 in Cologne, Germany, of a Jewish family. When Hitler came to power in January 1933 she could see the way the wind was blowing and in November of that year fled to England; she was admitted as a refugee. She later lost her German citizenship and became naturalised British. Her sister, Hannah, born in

1906, was not so lucky: she and her son, Edgar, who was born in 1938, were murdered by the Nazis in the Bergen-Belsen concentration camp. I believe Renata's mother had died from cancer. Her father, Hugo Israel, was born on 12 March 1876 (interestingly, John Symonds was also born on 12 March) in Hildesheim, Germany. As a widower he immigrated to the US in 1933, became a naturalised American in 1945, and died in 1950. In America he worked, presumably as a manager or partner, in a furniture and clothing store called Waldheim's.

Renata was only 20 years old when she came to Britain, alone and unable to speak a word of English. Her most precious possession was her violin. A customs officer, doubting that the violin was really hers, asked her to play it. This she did, to his satisfaction and enjoyment. After arrival in London she became an *au pair* and a nursery nurse. She met my father during the war and they married in 1945.

Our father's income as a writer was at times precarious, and our mother was the main breadwinner. She gained qualifications[11] in sociology and related disciplines, and in teaching, and until her retirement in 1978 was employed by the Inner London Education Authority as a remedial teacher for maladjusted children.

Thereafter, although having no formal training in psychotherapy she acquired extensive knowledge of the writings of C. G. Jung and worked as a psychotherapist in private practice from her home. She had a full workload of clients, many of whom she continued to see until her nineties. She also worked for two charitable organisations, the Highgate Counselling Centre and the Westminster Pastoral Foundation, as a therapist, supervisor, and trainer.

---

11 Under the auspices of the University of London these were: Certificate with Distinction in Social Structure and Social Conditions in England (1949); Certificate with Distinction in Social Psychology (1950); Certificate with Distinction in Social Philosophy (1951); Diploma in Criminology and the Psychology of Delinquency (1952); Teacher's Certificate with Distinction in the Theory and Practice of Education at the Infant School Stage (1955); Diploma in the Education of Maladjusted Children (1961).

***

Our parents were thus almost entirely without support from their own families in the difficult business of bringing up children. Further, they had to contend with the uncertainties of life in post-war Britain and had little money. Nonetheless, they did their best according to their lights and I don't think our childhoods in a material sense were exceptional for the time.

Was I jealous of my younger brother? Of course I was. There was the normal sibling rivalry, much exacerbated by the wrong-headed childbirth practices of the 1940s. New mothers were expected to 'rest' after delivery, if not actually stay in bed—the very worst thing you could do. It meant my mother disappeared for ten days when I was only eighteen months old and I was left to the tender care of my father. I refused to eat. Fearing that I would starve to death, he tried to force me to eat. I don't remember how this battle ended, but when at last my mother returned, she had a little usurper in her arms! I ignored her at first but gradually she succeeded in getting me to play with her.

In spite of this, as I recall, most of the time when my brother and I were growing up we got on reasonably well. Later we used to go on holidays together, once hitch-hiking to Corsica and another year to Scandinavia; we also went mountain walking in the Cairngorms in Scotland. In our twenties for a time we were quite close, even sharing a flat. So what went wrong? As mentioned in the Introduction, it is the object of this book to try to shed light on this question.

2
TOMMY'S EARLY LIFE

THE KIND OF person my brother became as an adult was prefigured in his behaviour as a child. The earliest memory I have of this was when I was about 6 years old. We lived in a flat comprising the basement and ground floor of a terraced house at 19 Arkwright Road, Hampstead, in north London. It was a pleasant place and we had use of the rear garden. It had been requisitioned by the local council because there was a shortage of housing after the war due to the bombing, and we were lucky enough to be offered this home. We lived there from around 1948 to 1953. The house was owned by a Polish gentleman called Stephan Konowski—we called him Norski—who lived in the upper part of the house. He was a man of short of stature who wore gold-rimmed spectacles and had a moustache. I rather liked him. He had a lady friend called Miss Diamond who visited regularly. We were quite poor in those days and couldn't afford much furniture so we made do with wooden orange boxes instead of chairs. When such properties were later de-requisitioned Norski wanted us to leave, so there was probably some friction between him and our parents.

In the basement of the front of the house we had a kitchen and dining room, and we could look up to the street level through the windows which were covered with net curtains. There was a door from the kitchen to the place where the dustbins were kept. One day Norski came down to empty his rubbish as we were sitting at breakfast, and our mother made a thoughtless remark to express her irritation with him for wanting his house back. She said, 'There's Norski, he's a silly little man.' She should not have said this in front of the children—or at least not in front of Tommy!

Later that day mother, brother, and I went out to the shops in Hampstead. It was sunny spring weather. After a while we met Norski coming down the hill in Ellerdale Road. He raised his hat to mother in a courteous greeting and they exchanged a few pleasantries. Then Tommy, with self-conscious glee, spoke up:

'Oh Norski, do you know, do you know what Mummy said about you?'

'No, what did your mother say about me?'

'She said, you're a *silly little man!*' Severe embarrassment. It was a moment that mother must have wished the ground would open up and swallow her. Norski was self-conscious about his height and it was this that upset him, not being called silly. He responded, 'Yes, yes, I am little.' I can't remember what my mother said after that or how it ended, but later she had to go and ring his doorbell to apologise to him. This incident became a piece of family folklore, ever after being referred to, of course, as 'Silly little man!'

Rise above it
Considering our father's own fatherless upbringing and my mother being an inexperienced young woman in a new country with no parents or siblings, it's not surprising they had difficulty bringing up their own children. I'm not saying they were bad parents— far from it. If I had any complaint about them it was that they were not strict enough. Their style of child rearing, however, could account for some of the difficulties Tommy encountered in later life. Was I not, then, equally affected? I like to think that I was intelligent enough to realise there was only one person I could rely on to make progress in life, and that was myself.

Our father had the ill-judged idea that he had to 'protect' Tommy from me. He called him by a baby name, 'Shmoogie', and he was often referred to as 'poor Shmoogie'. We were never allowed to fight. Being older and at that time bigger and stronger, father was afraid if we engaged in the normal rough and tumble of brothers the world over, I would seriously hurt him. Tommy, however, was quick to take advantage of this situation: he would deliberately provoke me—it was 'silly little man' all over again—knowing he could do so with impunity since our father would invariably intervene on his side. Naturally, I suffered a sense of injustice over this. Once I went to him with a story of a recent quarrel with Tommy, asking him to be a Solomon when he had heard it. I forget the details, but I told him that I did something, to which Tommy did something else, to which I reacted, etc. Now, please tell me, who was right and who was wrong? Without hesitation father pronounced that it was clear I was wrong and Tommy was right. Then I delivered my *dénouement*: I had reversed the names! This amounted to an admission that father had judged that *I* was in the right and *Tommy* was in the wrong! But no. My victory was short-lived. Without missing a beat father declared that, even so, since I was the elder and wiser, therefore I should *rise above it!* This was an impossible burden to impose on a small child. Did I resent my brother for this? No, I felt sorry for him that he had to resort to invoking our father's protection all the time instead of fighting his own battles.

Covered in bandages
Tommy milked this situation for all it was worth. Even when grown up he always relied on our father to help him deal with the many practical affairs of life that a responsible adult should take in his stride. He liked to play the role of victim, in which father apparently felt he needed to collude, so that he would receive sympathy and help. Poor Shmoogie thereby later acquired an extension to his baby name: *Covered in bandages!* It was a kind of family joke.

Although father seemed to realise at times that such over-indulgence was not good for Tommy, he seemed largely incapable of putting his foot down when it was needed and of standing up to him: telling him what was right and what was wrong. On occasion, though, father's patience was tried too far—but then he would make another joke of it: *Completely ruined his character!* Alas, many a true word is spoken in jest.

School and academic career

The protectiveness shown by our parents towards Tommy extended to his schooling. I went to a Church of England primary school from 1951 to 1955 called the Hampstead Parochial School, which I enjoyed. When aged 11, I took the Eleven Plus national examination, the result of which determined whether a child was deemed of sufficient academic standard to attend a Grammar school, or if not, he or she would go to what was called a Secondary Modern school. So that there wouldn't be overt competition between us, even though Tommy would have been in the year below me, he was sent to a nearby separate establishment, New End School. I couldn't understand this because I clearly remember I would have liked to have had my brother in the same school; it would have been fun and we could have supported one another in the usual playground fights! Tommy wasn't stupid—he later graduated from university (described hereunder)—but he didn't do so well in the Eleven Plus and went to a Secondary Modern school. But being unhappy at that place, father managed to get him transferred at the age of 13 to a Grammar school called Quintin Kynaston. He was unhappy there too, complaining that 'the teachers can't teach.' He left this school at 18 but without the requisite number of A levels to apply for university.

There was a way around this deficiency, however: he could take what were called Scottish Highers, the equivalent of A levels in England but reputed to be easier. It was admirable that he went on his own to Scotland for a couple of days to take these examinations, succeeded in acquiring two Scottish Highers, and that he subsequently obtained a place at Trinity College, Dublin, to study Classics (Latin and Greek). One problem remained: to be eligible for a grant for tuition fees and living expenses you needed *three* Highers, since only two were not considered to be equivalent to the two A levels in England which would suffice. Fortunately, father had a friend who held a high position in the London County Council, the institution which at that time had the power to bestow grants.

As a favour to father, he used his influence to push through Tommy's application.

All problems being solved, Tommy started his student life at the prestigious Trinity College. But was he happy? He was on a four year course, and the terms were only six weeks long. As soon as he arrived he sent plaintive letters home, always starting in the same way: 'I'm *so* unhappy....' By the middle of the term his mood had improved and towards the end of the term his letters reflected that he had got used to it: student life wasn't so bad after all. This sequence was repeated each term until he graduated with a Bachelor's degree, and subsequently he acquired an MA.

So what could Tommy do next? The only job he found open to him was teaching, but he hated this and after a couple of years gave it up. Then once more, father to the rescue. He thought Tommy might do well as an antiquarian book dealer and arranged for him to be apprenticed to an established dealer whom he knew. After that he gave him seed money to buy his own stock of books and set himself up independently. This wasn't a bad move, for Tommy eventually became a successful dealer in rare books; he also had a share in a publishing business which he went into with an Irish friend from university, Liam.

Tommy thus had much reason to be grateful to our father for supporting him throughout his educational career and helping him become established in life.

Overindulgence

Our parents' inability to draw a line with Tommy came to a head, with unfortunate consequences, in his late teenage years. He had met an extremely shy but rather sweet Dutch girl who was temporarily homeless. I don't know what she was doing in London. Now Tommy, in the days when we were growing up in our parents' flat (of which more will be said later), occupied a small bedroom off the kitchen. It had space only for a desk, chair, bookshelf, and—a double bed. He wanted his girlfriend to stay with him. I felt it was wrong for an obviously sexual relationship to be carried on under the noses of our parents—this was the 1960s—apart from practical considerations. But our parents, being unable to refuse Tommy anything, agreed, and she stayed for some weeks. Inevitably but hardly surprisingly, Dutch girlfriend became pregnant. What to do? Marriage was impossible, the child was unwanted, and abortion only became legal in Britain (excluding Northern Ireland) some years later in 1968. Nonetheless, with the help of another of father's useful friends, the pregnancy was terminated. Situation retrieved, but of course that relationship was then at an end.

Another of example of how overindulgence 'completely ruined his character' is the following: I was once walking with father in the countryside and for no particular reason he told me an incident to do with Tommy which rather annoyed me.

It was at a time when Tommy frequently moved house and gave the address where our parents were living as his forwarding address. Obviously, when you remove from a place of residence it is important that all the utility bills are paid up to date. But when he left this particular home in the east end of London he neglected to pay an outstanding electricity bill. The bill was forwarded to father's address. And what did father do? Did he pass the bill over to Tommy? Did he point out that if you fail to pay an overdue electricity bill without good reason, you are likely to be prosecuted, your credit rating may be compromised, and in any case you will be in bad odour with the electricity company so that they may not supply you with electricity in the future? No. *He paid the bill for him!* This, he told me, was in order to 'help' him. It wasn't as if Tommy was short of money, and I told him that this was not being helpful: it was *hindering* him—by depriving him of the opportunity of learning what happens if you don't pay your bills!

That wasn't the only bill of Tommy's that father paid. For example, over a period of something like three years, until he got fed up with it, he paid Tommy's son's private school fees. Again, it wasn't as if Tommy couldn't afford to pay them himself. At that time he had a nice house, a BMW car, and a thriving business as a publisher and antiquarian book dealer which involved regular trips to Europe and the US. Nonetheless, he preferred to inveigle our father, who was at that time living on his pension, to pay these fees for him. Father, being entrenched in the habit of giving Tommy everything he demanded and allowing his over-generous nature to be taken advantage of, agreed: the money was paid out of his bank account by standing order.

3

ACHES AND PAINS

IT IS MOST unfortunate that for much of his life poor Shmoogie suffered from a chronic physical complaint that he somewhat indelicately referred to as his 'balls ache' or, less indelicately, as his 'pains'. That is, from the age of 14 he was plagued by a testicular pain; later it affected his stomach as well. He consulted numerous doctors and specialists, both on the NHS and privately, and once even attended a pain clinic, but diagnosis and effective treatment were elusive.

This problem was elaborated in a letter to me from our father dated 1 November 1986:

> Tom yesterday went to see another specialist, one called Dr L— whom T called a psychiatrist; but he is also a physician and even a surgeon, so T said. And he put T on PARNATE[12]; this I don't like—I mean all this drugging. And Tom told me that when he is on PARNATE he mustn't eat certain foods such as cheese or drink more than a little alcohol. I'm distressed about the whole unending business; it goes on and on. I told him to see Marianne Jacoby[13] but he thinks his stomach pains are purely physical and he wants to find an organic cause. I told him that what he is suffering from is depression and his guts ache is a symptom of the depression.

Three days later a follow-up arrived:

---

[12] An antidepressant, not used these days as a first-line treatment; it has many side-effects and dietary restrictions need to be observed.
[13] A psychotherapist and graphologist friend, the widow of the above-mentioned Hans Jacoby.

Tommy received this morning a bill from Dr L— for *one* consultation; that seemed to me pretty steep. T feels terrible in the morning, he says; this I think is owing to the drugs he is taking, prescribed by Dr L—, who strikes me as a charlatan. In my last letter I mentioned the name of the drug which I've since forgotten. I told him to *stop* taking these drugs; this merely puts him in a rage with me. He feels so terrible, he feels so ill, he contemplates suicide; it goes on and on. I try to point out to him that he will never be cured as long as he will only see his trouble as a bodily thing, and will not even consider that his personality may play a part. He wants a doctor to pin-point it by saying, yes, there is a cancer of something equally terrible, then he will be relieved because there would be a chance of a cure. I won't have any of this, and so our discussion—which he always involves me in—ends in a row. I never introduce into our conversation his 'illness'; he is the one to bring it up and if I've told him what I think once I've told him a hundred times. At the moment he is with Marianne Jacoby whom I've persuaded him to see. Perhaps she can knock some sense into him. I had a word with her beforehand, putting her in the picture. A 'pain' which one has had for twenty years and which never develops into anything that would be medically interesting is, in my view, a pain which one should be able easily to bear. T can't see this. I don't believe in this pain or in this illness but I do believe in his depression. The source of the trouble is in his psyche, his personality.

Shortly after, another letter:

Tommy: I do my best; he goes up and down, more downs than ups. I've not known him like it before. He'll come out of it (I believe) and be the better for it. I am sure he is grateful for your ministrations.

Next, a very perceptive letter (Plate 1) on the matter dated 15 November 1986:

> Tommy: he would drive you potty, as he almost drives me. He easily succumbs to tears, and is full of regrets about pretty well everything. That is on the one hand. On the other he is stubborn to the point of perversity. It is not that he hasn't the brains or the energy to do this or that which he should do or must do; it is that he won't—just to be bloody-minded. Hence his stomach pains. I've told him a thousand times to give up taking tablets and running to doctors for only he can cure himself by one of two methods or both: enduring the conflict, or waiting to see what will come out of it; not prolonging the conflict by failing to face it—that extends the neurosis. And by doing the things, such as paying his bills, which he knows he ought to do but won't. If he did this, he'd shed his resentment. He relapses into babyhood, to which I said, 'Well, that's all right *as long as you know what you are doing.*'
>
> Because of the turmoil he has been in, he has, I believe, learnt a lot (which he won't admit of course) and is in some ways already a nicer person. The problem is, I think, to free himself from the childhood psyche; there is a greater personality waiting in the wings to emerge.[14] But meanwhile, oh dear oh dear, he goes on and on. For the last few nights he has slept here and in the morning he greets me with the remark that he is as bad as ever. It is not true and he had admitted that, suddenly and for no reason, his pains have gone, but they come back. His so-called pains are his reason for remaining stuck. That is why I don't believe in his pains no matter what he says.
>
> I've written this about T because you are concerned and I want to put you in the picture to the best of my ability.

---

[14] These remarks shed much light on the problems described in this book. Why could Tommy not free himself from his childhood psyche?

In my view the problem with father's approach was that he was attempting to cure Tommy of his pains by providing psychological awareness from the outside; that is, he told Tommy what he believed underlied his problems. I would agree with this, but to effect a cure, or at least come to terms with the problem, understanding has to come from *within*. If I had a patient like this I would ask him to tell me his dreams; what is going on in his unconscious that might shed some light on these unbearable pains? One might even suggest that he should ask himself why he *needs* them. It seemed he did indeed in a sense need them to avoid having to face up to the responsibilities and struggles of adult life. Father was not a psychotherapist but even so his insight was considerable. On the other hand, mother *was* a highly experienced therapist, thoroughly conversant with the works of C. G. Jung. I know she did dream analysis with her clients but am unaware whether she attempted this with Tommy. Even so, such treatment is much better left to an objective outsider. For example, mother could have insisted he didn't call her late at night and instead should take his troubles to an independent therapist. Apart from Marianne Jacoby, I know he saw a Jungian analyst and there may have been others who tried to help him with psychotherapy. Unfortunately, it seemed that none of this was of much help and I can only conclude he found it more comfortable to remain emotionally dependent on our parents. This is shown by the fact that, as related above, even after having had a good talk with father, he needed to stay with our parents for a few nights in their home. I think the seeds of this dependency were sown in childhood and then became entrenched. But I wondered whether his habit of affecting rudeness—'please' and 'thank you' were not in his vocabulary—was his way of unconsciously straining to break these unhealthy bonds. It was as if he was begging his parents to *draw the line*. Unfortunately, they were unable to do this except in moments of extreme exasperation. Thus, they unwittingly encouraged him to remain tied to them in a child-like emotional state. I'm not suggesting they should have cast him adrift, but some boundaries could and should have been made clear.

Another insightful letter arrived on 2 December 1986:

> Tommy: he continues to complain about his *stomach pains* which I find impossible to believe in because his behaviour is *not at all* like that of someone in physical pain. I am *not* saying that he has *nothing* to complain about; he obviously has, but in my view it is not physical in the ordinary sense. Besides, he has had his 'stomach pains' investigated by several doctors; and Dr S—, a specialist, who may be as ignorant as a stone, could only come up with 'spasmodic colon'; later he confessed he was *baffled* by Tommy's pains. T's description of these pains as 'unendurable' and 'continuous' is obviously wrong, for during our discussion about his difficulties which include his pains, he forgets about them, and his behaviour is normal, i.e., he is obviously in no pain at all. Now, his attitude towards his pains is not that of a man, but that of a whining baby—I'm sorry to put it so bluntly. A man can put up with a certain amount of pain, Tommy can't. Furthermore, a man can carry on to some extent with his work. T can't, but in fact he does get on with this and that and hasn't taken to his bed. *He takes refuge in his pains.* There are many things wrong with Tommy, his life is in a mess in some areas (but not in all) but he doesn't want to look at that, and when I mention that, he promptly replies, 'I can't do anything about that because I'm in *such terrible pain.*' So we go round and round and get nowhere. 'If only I were free from these pains!' he cries, to which I reply, 'These pains are your best friend. Ask them what they want from you.' And I add, 'If it weren't for these pains you'd be nothing. These pains come to solve your problem; they go to the heart of the matter, but don't try to push them away from you as if you're perfectly all right and it's only these terrible pains which have upset your apple

cart.'[15] In general, since these pains have begun, he's *improved as a person*. Could they be birth pains? I'm telling you all this because when you arrive at Heathrow [on an impending visit from Japan] Tommy will be there, waiting for an opportunity to give you a long account of his *unending and unendurable misery*.

The stomach pain is possibly an identification with father who used to complain of his 'guts ache' which he recognised was due to eating too quickly. Nonetheless, it was bad enough for father to have had it investigated with endoscopy (stomach camera): the result was normal. Tommy's stomach pain, like that in his testicle, was undiagnosable by eminent specialists, but the prescription of Parnate implies a psychological cause.

I did my best to help Tommy with the problem of his pains and once suggested he should try acupuncture, referring him to a colleague I knew in London who offered this treatment under the Health Service. Tommy did not, however, take up the offer. The following emails, of which the first (30 January 2003) is from the acupuncturist, Dr C—, explain why:

> Thank you for sending details of your brother's condition. Unfortunately, I have not been able to talk to him directly, and I am sorry to report that he has rather upset our office staff. They claim that he has been rude and demanding on the telephone in insisting that I telephone him. He even called one of them 'stupid' I am told.
>
> I did indeed try to call him on two occasions during my busy clinic yesterday, but the number was first engaged and later not answered. I am sure you will understand that my

---

15 These remarks echo a diary entry of Ludwig Wittgenstein's in 1948: 'Don't let this grief vex you. You should let it into your heart. Nor should you be afraid of madness. It comes to you perhaps as a friend and not as an enemy, and the only thing that is bad is your resistance. Let grief into your heart. Don't lock the door on it. Standing outside the door, in the mind, it is frightening, but in the heart it is not.' Quoted in Ray Monk, *Wittgenstein: the Duty of Genius*, Jonathan Cape, 1990, p 534.

schedule is such that I cannot routinely offer to call patients back.

I understand his condition probably puts an undue stress on him, however, I must consider the well-being of our committed staff, and whilst I am loathe to take such action, I must withdraw my offer to see him as a patient of the — Clinic.

I replied as follows, and forwarded the whole correspondence to Tommy:

> Thank you for your message. I fully understand your action and I do not blame you in the slightest. I am only sorry, and embarrassed, that my brother has put you in this situation and I wish to apologise on his behalf to you and your staff for any unpleasantness that he has caused.

Unfortunately, there was nothing unusual about this incident. In the hope that our mother might have some good influence—a forlorn hope!—I also sent the correspondence to her, with a covering letter:

> Since you know all about T's problems, he will doubtless have told you (and probably complained about me in the process) that I have tried to find an acupuncturist for him in the hope that it will help his pains. I went to some trouble to find and communicate with a doctor I thought might be able to help him and who was willing to see him. All that T needed to do was to telephone for an appointment in the normal way. So what does he do? Upsets everyone and puts himself at a disadvantage.
>
> No doubt you will hear furious complaints about my attitude and the attitude of the staff at the acupuncture clinic, etc. Perhaps, instead of sympathising with poor hard-done-by Tommy, you might use your influence to point out that this sort of behaviour is unacceptable.

He has upset other doctors to whom I have introduced him, for example Dr R— and Dr V—. It is only because they are good-natured and because of their relationship with me that they have put up with him, but they were not happy with his demanding and rude behaviour.

What, then, was the cause of the pains, particularly the testicular pain? Its alleged persistence and severity, in the absence of any detectable physical disorder, make one indeed wonder about a psychological overlay. I would myself from time to time see men complaining of testicular pain. Having excluded obvious disease, a reasonable assumption would be that it was due to non-specific inflammation of the prostate gland; a trial of antibiotic treatment sometimes helped. Prostatitis can be acquired from sexual contact, but I presume Tommy was a virgin when it started at age 14. Later he told me he sometimes visited prostitutes. I remember saying to him that such activity couldn't be very satisfying because you have no personal relationship with a prostitute. 'That's just the point,' he said, 'you have no relationship with them!'

In Tommy's case, in spite of the absence of a diagnosis, he had been treated empirically with an antidepressant, Parnate, and I believe at another time he took gabapentin, a drug for neuropathic pain, again without benefit.

If there was a psychological component, how might it have arisen? Pain is a symptom: it tells you something is wrong. There certainly was something wrong in Tommy's case, but he never would ask himself what it might be. He was stuck with the pain, and could not progress to consider what it might have been trying to draw his attention to.

A striking feature of Tommy's personality was his emotional dependency on our parents together with a stubborn insistence that they *must* do this or that for him. He would never take 'No' for an answer but would incessantly nag and pester them. This applied particularly to the problem of the pains which it seemed he used as a stick to beat them with. What did he hope to gain by constantly telling them of his symptoms? I can only guess that at some level he was demanding they should relieve him of the pain, as if it was *their fault* he was suffering so much.

One is reminded of a child throwing a tantrum whose parents refuse to buy him an ice-cream or give in to some other demand. I can hear our father saying, 'Anything for peace' sake!' I also wonder what it was about that John Symonds quarrelled so often and vociferously with *his* father on the stairs at 7 Bruton Street. Certainly, John found it difficult to 'stand the tension,' as he would say, of quarrelling with Tommy, though very occasionally he reached the end of his tether and told him to go away. Then, a short time later, he would be calling to invite him round for supper! In these disagreements mother would usually take Tommy's side; they would rarely present a united front.

There is an echo of this in the above-quoted letter from RWS to John: 'I will not, however, listen to the raving of a young man whose temper gets the better of him because he is unable to get his own way in everything…' Yet this is exactly what father did with Tommy: he listened almost endlessly to the ravings, or rather, whinings, of a young man whose temper frequently got the better of him, until he often *did* get his own way!

At one point, however, I heard that it became so bad that father for some months forbade Tommy to call at their home. But mother entered into a conspiracy with poor Shmoogie: she would entertain him secretly and listen his troubles, unbeknown to father. Then things went back to their usual pattern.

4

GIRLFRIENDS

TOMMY'S RELATIONSHIPS WITH women were often problematic. Was he just unlucky or was there something in him which caused the difficulties? From my own observations and from what father related to me, it seemed that Tommy's attitude to women was a reflection of his attitude to the world in general.

To illustrate this I need to go back to 1975 when I acquired my first home, a flat comprising the upper three floors of a house in Belsize Lane near the fashionable Hampstead area of London. I was offered this opportunity by the then tenant (the landlord was the Church Commissioners), a friend of father's, who wanted to move out and who, for a consideration, was able to have the lease assigned to me. Later I was lucky enough to be able to purchase a ninety-nine year lease on this flat for a nominal sum.

Thinking it would be lonely on my own and as there was enough space I invited Tommy to move in with me. We were up till then living with our parents. I was working as a doctor and Tommy was in the antiquarian book business. We were both bachelors at the time. After some months of sharing my home (for which he paid me a peppercorn rent) Tommy acquired a girlfriend, called Rosemary. As she seemed to be homeless Tommy asked her to live with him in my flat. I made no objection and, on the contrary, thought a female presence would cheer the place up. She might even be more efficient at housework that we were! To start with all went well, but then a problem arose. We took turns to use the kitchen, which was also the dining room, for our evening meals. If Tommy and Rosemary used it first they often left the plates, pots and pans, etc., without doing the washing up. I then needed to speak to Tommy about this matter—which should never have arisen in the first place—but he was unconcerned and suggested I talk with Rosemary. I did so. 'Rosemary,' I said, 'after you've had your dinner will you please do the washing up straightaway.' Her response: 'Fuck off!' I did not reply to this gratuitous rudeness but had to tell Tommy that Rosemary was no longer welcome in my home. Did he apologise for her behaviour and promise in future the washing up would be promptly performed? No. He was annoyed with *me* for what he saw as *my* unreasonable behaviour! It led to a major row between us and it was a struggle to get them both to leave. When this was achieved I was then on my own but at least could live in peace.

There is a post-script to this incident. After leaving Belsize Lane, Tommy acquired a rented flat of his own in the Holland Park area of London where he and Rosemary moved in together. However, not long after they quarrelled. Why was that? Because Rosemary got tired of Tommy and invited a new boyfriend to live with her in a spare room in Tommy's flat! Then Tommy, similarly, found it difficult to get rid of his unwelcome lodgers. Although it sounded like poetic justice he didn't deserve to be treated like that. Later we made up our quarrel and re-established normal fraternal relations—for a while.

Thereafter he lived for a time in a flat in the Little Venice area of London with an Irishwoman called Mairead; she had a somewhat strong personality. One day I had occasion to call upon Tommy at about 10.00 in the morning. I rang the bell and he let me in. Mairead was still in bed, and seeing me through the partially open bedroom door as I passed by to the living room, called out, 'What are you doing here so early? Fuck off!'

Another of his girlfriends whom I met, Louise, was an American with rather brash manners and a lack of familiarity with English ways. Once we were all enjoying Christmas lunch together with our parents. After the main course a Christmas pudding was produced which father had made according to an old traditional recipe. When the pudding was placed on the table having been steamed for three hours, she suddenly stuck her finger right into the pudding and announced in her loud American accent, 'It's hot!' Another family joke. What was not so funny was what Tommy told me when that relationship ended. Although he was quite sad when she left, he described her, not as his lover or girlfriend, but as 'The best fuck I've ever had!'

It appeared to me that Tommy had little genuine interest in other people; he was much more concerned with what *they* could do for *him*, or with what he could get out of them. He used girlfriends largely in order to *complain* to them. Endlessly. That is, as in the case of our parents, to complain about how badly life was treating him, and how unfair it was that he had difficulties in his business, and with his health, and especially with me. That meant he needed someone to *blame* for all his problems: in particular, his parents for not sending him to the 'right' school, and for not teaching him about masturbation (!); and most of all he blamed *me* as the first-born for being *nasty* to him!

In this connection, there is a wonderful book about His Holiness the Dalai Lama called *The Art of Happiness* by Dr Howard Cutler, in which, among other pearls of wisdom, it is pointed out that if you seek someone or something to blame for your problems, it is a sure-fire recipe for an unhappy life. I was so impressed when I read this book that I sent Tommy a copy. Was he pleased to receive it? Did it help him to overcome his unhappiness? No, it made him worse: he took it entirely the wrong way and accused me of mocking him. Unfortunately, it seemed he was unable to progress in the three steps needed to acquire a little wisdom: first, blame your parents; next, blame yourself; finally, blame nobody.

A succession of other girlfriends followed and sooner or later he would introduce them to our parents, presumably seeking their approval. Although father was unfailingly courteous to these women face-to-face, when they had gone he felt constrained to tell Tommy his opinion: 'When I saw X my *face fell*. I wouldn't care to have her as a daughter-in-law!'

Mother, naturally, was annoyed at such criticism and urged him not to say these things to Tommy. She wanted to nurture the relationship, however unsuitable it seemed, even referring to it as a 'delicate little flower' that was not to be disturbed by any adverse criticism.

Then, as our father mentions in his own life, Providence intervened. Tommy met a woman called Maureen. She was from a different background and they shared little in their outlook and interests; she also smoked. Tommy began an affair with her and they lived together for a time; then they quarrelled and separated. However, one night a little while later, Tommy was feeling *lonely*. So what does he do? He visits Maureen and spends the night with her. I'll now quote from a letter father sent to me in Japan dated 2 July 1985:

> Maureen is pregnant, something which I was afraid would happen. It has not been confirmed by any test—a fortnight overdue with some morning sickness. What to do? Well, terminate it; but the latest thing I hear is that she doesn't want to in spite of being on very bad terms with Tommy. He blundered right into that situation, and when he thought he was shut of her! It tears me (and Mummy too) apart.
>
> I don't know what is going to happen. She has moved back to her first flat which flat she says she doesn't like any more. She has no, or few, friends.
>
> Fate has caught up with Tommy.
>
> On the whole—and by 'the whole' I mean the lack of love between them, and Maureen's instability (Tom calls her an insanely jealous baby)—I'm in favour of terminating the pregnancy. But if Maureen doesn't want to, I feel it would be wrong, ethically, to pressure her. And who knows what good may come out of this bad situation?
>
> I had a chat this morning with T on the telephone and what I said amounts to this: although I was completely against her having the child, I can't continue to be in the face of her wish to have it. I am not that sort of man, and in any case it

doesn't depend on me. Not having spoken to Maureen I don't know what she thinks, and she probably doesn't know what she thinks on this matter. She has only or mainly feelings of hatred for T.

The latest stage, I gather, is that T will fix up an appointment for her at a respectable clinic, to which clinic or hospital she'll go or not go. It's a volatile situation.

I always tell you everything but there's nothing you can do, and I don't think there's any advice that you can give which hasn't already been given. They are both in a great conflict about it. They both behaved like children.

It has thrown me into a gloom of course.

Although they subsequently never again lived together, a son, Toby, was born to Maureen, and as far as I can tell Tommy has had a good relationship with him. I say 'as far as I can tell' because, as will be shown in more detail later, Tommy kept him at a distance from me and doubtless poisoned his mind against me—his one and only uncle!

True love at last?
When Tommy reached his forties still a bachelor he decided it was time to find a wife. To my knowledge on two occasions he proposed to unsuitable women to whom he gave an engagement ring. In both cases it ended soon after in a horrible row with the ring being flung across the room! Then he had a lucky break—or so it seemed at first.

We have already met Tommy's university friend, Liam. His speciality was Armenian culture and language and he regularly visited Armenia—it was part of the Soviet Union up till 1989. Unfortunately, he suffered from a major disability, alcoholism, although to his credit he eventually managed to overcome it. On one of his trips to Armenia he had a drunken fling with a woman he picked up, and in the throes of passion offered her marriage. When he had sobered up he regretted this but could not go back on his word. In those days it was a serious matter to apply for an exit visa from the workers' paradise for any reason. You would lose your job and might find yourself persecuted in other ways. Being a decent man he felt obliged to follow through on his promise. Thus they married shortly after and she came to Britain as his wife. The marriage did not last but she had achieved her aim of acquiring British citizenship. Now, this woman had a friend in Yerevan (the capital of Armenia) to whom she offered to introduce Tommy. He jumped at the chance and hurried off to Yerevan as soon as he obtained a visa.

The friend, Anahita, known as Anna, was a charming lady, a medical doctor whose father, Professor Zohrabian, apparently was a famous neurosurgeon. Anna, at the time she met Tommy, was said to be aged 39 though it later turned out, as I heard, that she had been this age for about the previous five years. It was love at first sight. They might have met a second time before wedding preparations were put in hand. I remember telling Tommy that since it was well known that Soviet women would try to entrap western men to get out of the USSR, he should wait a bit longer before committing himself. Well, he wasn't going to take any advice from me and I was not invited to the wedding. But our father went and was fêted by the family during the jollifications which went on for three days. So Tommy was married at last. They seemed to get on well at first and maybe Anna to start with did have some real feelings for Tommy. She was certainly encouraged by our father who could speak a little Russian—he studied the language because of his love of Russian literature. But I am sorry to say they didn't live happily ever after.

On one occasion in the early 1990s I was invited to their flat in Kensington with our parents for lunch. It was a magnificent lunch. The table was covered with a variety of delicious food and soon I was pretty much full. Then the main course appeared!

At that time I was in the process of emigrating and had arranged to send some furniture, books, etc., from London to set up home in Japan. Now Tommy had a bicycle, a splendid racing machine, which he had not ridden for years and it seemed had no intention of using in the future; it was merely gathering dust in a storage cupboard where our parents lived. I asked him if I could have this bicycle and, if he would agree, have it added to the goods which were shortly due to be sent by air freight to Japan. Yes, I could have it—for payment. Anna interjected: 'Tommy, we don't charge our own family!' Later she took me aside and complained, 'Tommy is so infantile!' There was little I could say to raise her spirits. Then in due course the goods arrived. Was the bicycle included? Of course it was not.

The crack in the facade of their marriage widened after another incident. Tommy was by then established as an antiquarian book dealer and kept his stock of valuable books in their Kensington flat. One day he was visiting our parents when there was a panic phone call from Anna. She had been mugged and there had been an attempted robbery! He drove like a maniac from Belsize Lane to Kensington and arrived back home. Entering the flat, he brushed past Anna, who was in a distraught state, to check his valuable books. Great relief—the books were undisturbed! Then, and only then, did he turn to his poor wife. Two masked men had rung the doorbell pretending they had come to deliver flowers. When she opened the door they forced their way in and demanded money. She refused and was pushed around but not seriously hurt. Eventually they left empty-handed. Whatever the truth of the suggestion that Tommy was more concerned about his books than the safety and well-being of his wife, this distressing incident didn't help their relationship.

Anna's parents and younger sister were able to visit her in London after the Soviet Union collapsed in 1989. Our father wrote an account of a dinner party he gave, or rather, tried to give, for Anna, her parents, and Tommy on 5 February 1995. He called it 'A Day in the Life of John Symonds'. I reproduce it verbatim:

The day of the party for the Zohrabian family. I'd asked Anna if she would prefer to come on Saturday or Sunday. We agreed that it should be Sunday. I bought a bottle of champagne, a bottle of vodka—the Professor drinks only vodka, not wine—a whole large salmon, a pound of thinly sliced smoked ham (for our honoured guests, not for Renata or me), a variety of vegetables, etc. Renata was busy during the morning. After a very light lunch we began to prepare the feast, the last course of which was Xmas pudding, ice-cream, various cheeses. Guests to arrive at 7.00. At 5.00 the Professor (who is staying in Tom's large flat) telephoned to say he couldn't come. 'Well, fuck you!' I said in an angry voice. 'Why didn't you tell me this yesterday? What am I to do with all the food? The fish won't keep. I shall have to put it in the dustbin!' I rang off. He rang back about a quarter of an hour later to say that he and his incredibly stupid wife, Lola, who haunts Tom's flat like a ghoul, would come after all. We continued the cooking.

At 6.45 Tom, the Professor, and Lola arrived. The champagne was uncorked, the bottle of vodka taken out of the fridge, and we sat in the drawing room to drink and chat. It is the Professor's habit to take charge of everything, no matter whose house he is in. He seized the champagne bottle to top up my and Renata's glass without asking if we wanted it recharged. He talks but doesn't listen.

At 7.30, feeling hungry and there being no sign of Anna, I said, 'Let's eat.' We went to the kitchen and the feast began. We ate less than half of the salmon; there were so many other dishes, mainly vegetables. We came to the pudding stage. I poured brandy on the heated Xmas pudding and lit it. The Professor proposed yet another meaningless and insincere toast. No Anna. She obviously wasn't coming, but why hadn't she telephoned to say so?

We returned to the drawing room. The Professor dominated the conversation. I found his remarks so boring that after a while I went back to the kitchen to do the washing up.

Renata thought this rude of me, but when she came into the kitchen and saw that all the plates, knives, forks, dishes, and glasses had been washed up and put away, and all the left-over food put into the fridge, she forgot about my ill manners; she returned to the drawing room.

In came the Professor to the kitchen. 'I want to talk to you, John,' he said. 'Well, talk.' He had two main topics. 1. How stingy Tom, his son-in-law, is; 2, that I, as *loco parentis*, must tell Anna how to behave towards her husband. I listened to this drivel until I could stand it no longer; then I said, 'Anna is not a little girl of five! I can't tell her how to behave towards her husband, and you can be certain that I shan't. As for your remarks about Tom's meanness, will you give me an instance of it?' The instance he came up with concerned his other daughter, Nana, and it occurred about two years ago when she was visiting London. Tom, allegedly, had left Nana in his car while he went somewhere, and a traffic warden stuck a notice of a £50 fine on the windscreen. When Tom returned and learnt what had happened, he was furious and demanded £50 from Nana. The Professor hadn't been there and he had obviously muddled the incident up. The fine in any case wouldn't have been £50. I couldn't be bothered to tell the Professor that Tom had put up Nana in his flat for a whole year, and that he had taken Anna to California, Ireland, Germany, Poland, Moscow, and Italy, always staying in the top hotels; he'd paid £5,000 for Anna's medical treatment; and only the other day he'd given Souren, the Professor's grandson who is staying there, £500 as he was hard up. And recently he'd given Anna £15,000 which enables her to rent a small flat in St John's Wood; it is her bolthole. Hardly stinginess at that.

The Professor doesn't listen to what you say anyhow, only to what *he* says. As for the £20 fine for the car being in the wrong place, it was Anna who insisted that Nana should pay for it for being lazy or indifferent. Tom drove his parents-in-law back to his flat at 9.30. Where was Anna? Why hadn't she turned up?

This account shows two things: first, Tommy's laziness or dismissive attitude to authority by leaving his car in a place where parking is forbidden. And what was Nana supposed to do when a traffic warden approached? Begged and pleaded, or rushed off to try to find Tommy before the ticket was written? Second, it is interesting that Tommy had paid a considerable sum for Anna to have a bolthole. Later the truth emerged: she had left Tommy and was living there with her Armenian lover! The £15,000 and the other sums he lavished on her—clearly he wasn't hard-up—were a pathetic attempt to buy her love and persuade her to return to him after the marriage broke down.

It is also clear that the invitation to this wonderful feast, for which our parents went to such trouble and expense, was accepted under false pretences. I suspect a major row was going on between Anna's parents, Anna, and Tommy before the Professor's phone call to cancel their attendance; and Anna, with her Armenian lover waiting in the bolthole to cuckold Tommy, probably couldn't face being harangued by her own parents and her in-laws and with Tommy egging them on, to get her to behave properly towards her husband! Nonetheless, it is understandable that John didn't want the vodka-swilling Professor telling him to tell Anna how to behave, although he appears in his heavy-handed way to have meant well.

What is unclear to me is whether Anna went into the marriage in good faith, or whether she held Tommy in contempt from the start, merely making use of him to escape the Soviet Union. If the latter, it is explicable, though hardly excusable, because in order to survive if you lived behind the Iron Curtain prior to the fall of communism, it seemed lying and corruption were necessary to survive.

Whatever its origin, Anna's deviousness and conspiratorial nature are shown further in the next chapter.

5
PROBLEMS

WHEN IT WAS clear that I was going to make my life in Japan, the question arose of what to do with my flat in Belsize Lane. At first I let it for rent, but this turned out to be more trouble than it was worth, so I invited my parents to move there since it was much better than their own place. I did this purely for love and affection and asked for no rent. They merely paid the utilities, service charge, local taxes, and maintenance. The place they lived previously and where we grew up was in nearby West Hampstead on the first floor of a block of flats called Lyncroft Mansions, at No 66. When our parents moved to my home, they decided to assign the lease of No 66 (they owned a long leasehold) to Tommy. But for reasons of tax avoidance, Tommy asked them to put it in the name of his wife, Anna. This was a risky strategy: what if they later fell out? In spite of that obvious concern, Anna's name was used.

Thus Tommy acquired a nice flat free of charge which he used mainly as an office. He worked there with his partner, Liam. It was, however, against the terms of the lease to use the premises to run a business.

At first the arrangement worked well. But then problems arose. To start with, Liam, who had little consideration for others and was a 'night bird', used his noisy IBM golf ball typewriter to bang away in the middle of the night. The neighbours complained. He told them to get lost. They complained to the management. Management told Tommy he was in breach of the lease and he had to leave. Then there was another problem. Anna, as the nominal leaseholder, had a key. One fine day she moved in, changed the locks, and refused to let Tommy or Liam enter the place. Panic. An injunction was sought and obtained, giving Tommy access. But the marriage by this stage had irretrievably broken down. The only question remaining was how much Tommy would have to pay to divorce his wife, who was ever after politely referred to by him as 'that bitch'. The suit came up for a hearing. On the steps of the court Tommy offered £60,000. Not enough. Well, let the court decide. The court did so: £40,000. Anna in her greed got merely two-thirds of what was originally offered. But that wasn't the end of the matter. Tommy hadn't got £40,000, so apart from being under pressure to leave No 66 for breaching the lease, he had to sell the flat for a knock-down price to pay Anna off. It is very sad that all this could have been avoided if Tommy had not rushed into marriage with a woman he hardly knew, and had used a bit of common sense not to annoy the neighbours in the middle of the night.

Auntie Eleanor
Father's sister, our aunt Eleanor, was very fond of Tommy and me. She lived south of the River Thames in the Lewisham area of London and let out part of her house to a dental practice. She never married but for a long time lived with a man called Tracy who was a dentist. I remember meeting him when they visited us in Arkwright Road. He had a moustache and smoked a pipe. He was a married man but separated. Unfortunately he died from a heart attack. Apart from Tracy, Eleanor loved dogs and always had a Dachshund which she called Jasper. Her life was quite full and she had many friends especially in Lincolnshire where she often went. When she was older she moved to Tunbridge Wells and lived in quiet respectability in a detached suburban house. Father and she were close. In her old age she didn't have much money. Father would give her something when he could afford to and for a time I also contributed to her financial welfare. To boost her income she re-mortgaged her house; it would be repaid on her death from the sale of the house, the residue falling to her estate.

When Tommy learnt of this he was furious. He said if she was hard up he could have paid her a stipend. He wanted as much as possible from her estate when the time came and did not want its value to be reduced by something as extravagant as a second mortgage! My attitude was that this was none of our business; Auntie Eleanor could do with her own property what she pleased and didn't have to ask anyone's permission.

In 1997 at the age of 86, Auntie Eleanor passed away from stomach cancer. In her will she bequeathed her estate in equal shares to Tommy and me.

However, her body was hardly cold when Tommy rushed around to her house and on some pretext gained entry. He had come in a hired van to remove certain property he wanted, which he carted away. But before probate was granted he had no right to do this. The main items to which he helped himself (two beds and a few other pieces of furniture) were of little value, but they had to be taken into account when it came to disposing of the estate. The solicitor dealing with the matter found Tommy's behaviour embarrassing, if not illegal, and she asked me if I wanted to deduct the value of the property that had been removed from Tommy's share of the cash he would receive. I declined this offer.

Why, oh why, did Tommy behave in this undignified and greedy way? Was he afraid of *missing* something? Did he believe he was *entitled* to grab as much as possible from our poor recently deceased aunt's home? Was he *resentful* because she had re-mortgaged her house? Or was it perhaps an echo of the attitude he acquired when he was a small boy and was allowed at the family Christmas lunch to pile his plate so high that he could only eat half of what he had taken? Or rather, if he had never been taught what was permissible and what was not, how could he be expected to know the difference?

The Dictionary dispute

When I was living in Tokyo with my family, my parents would come to see us about once a year. On one such visit in 1990 they brought with them the two volumes of Dr Samuel Johnson's famous *Dictionary of the English Language*, a first edition published in 1755. Father had bought it at auction for a modest price. It was in good condition but needed a new binding which he arranged. He hoped to sell it for a handsome profit to a Japanese book dealer. We tried with a large firm called Maruzen but they weren't interested. As my parents didn't want to take these two heavy volumes (12 kg in total) all the way back to London they left them with me. I kept them carefully and even insured them.

Then there was a courteous letter from father, 12 November 1990, saying:

> I forgot to ask you if you will bring with you [on a forthcoming visit to London], if it is not inconvenient for you to do so, those two volumes of Johnson's *Dictionary*. Of course, if you'd rather keep them for your own use and amusement, please do so. But if you don't particularly want them, I think I can sell them…and give you the money!

This was followed by a letter dated 16 December 1990:

> The Johnson *Dictionary*; upon closer inspection and after hearing what Tommy and [a friend] had to say, I found it to be *no good*; it was misdescribed in Sotheby's catalogue. So, hopefully, I shall be able or rather Tommy will be able to return it; it's not yet been paid for.

Did father intend to give me the *Dictionary* or did the later message mean that he wanted me to bring it back to London? I assumed the former. In either event there was no further mention of it until *fifteen years later* when out-of-the-blue a demand arrived from Tommy to return it. All right, if he would pay the postage and reimburse what I had expended in insuring it, I would send it to him. Of course he wouldn't agree to that—he expected my wife to act as a courier and bring it with her on a pending visit to London. I guessed this demand meant that Tommy might have paid half the purchase cost, in which case for simplicity I said I would buy him out by reimbursing his share. Would he agree to this? Of course not.

Although it was clear that the *Dictionary* was not as valuable as it had seemed initially, Tommy was suddenly *obsessed*—there is no other word for it—to get his hands on it. There were despairing messages from father: 'Tommy is bullying me over the *Dictionary*.' Even mother joined in, begging me to return the *Dictionary*. Clearly she had been put up to this by Tommy; it was beginning to cause a rift between our mother and me as shown in a letter I felt constrained to write her on 27th June 2005:

> I apologise for having to write to you in these terms. It caused me great distress that you enlivened my evening the other day by your and Daddy's telephone call, not to tell me something interesting or important about the family, but to raise yet again this wretched business of the *Dictionary*. It was particularly painful to hear you in the background egging Daddy on: 'Go on, tell him you want the *Dictionary* back!'
>
> Daddy has already made it perfectly clear when he spoke to me on the telephone about three weeks ago—he does have moments when he is lucid and forthright—that he does *not* want the *Dictionary* back and that I may keep it.
>
> One of the luxuries of being a grandparent, surely, is that the responsibility for child rearing is behind you. If one of your children (or grandchildren) is inconsiderate enough to try to involve you in contentious matters, you should simply decline.

The mystery of the true ownership of the *Dictionary* is explained in a handwritten note (Plate 2) among some of father's papers that were sent to me after his death. It reads as follows:

> Tom owes me £530.
> £780 ÷ 2 = £390 + £110 rebinding = £500
> Therefore Tom owes me £30 which sum he paid on 10 Jan 80
> We are now quits and the dictionary belongs to me.

In other words, father paid the cost of the *Dictionary* and rebinding himself. He and Tommy were going to share the cost of the purchase, but then Tommy couldn't or didn't want to pay his share plus the cost of rebinding, a total of £500. He already owed father £530 for something else. He paid the difference of £30 and the remaining £500 was paid in kind by letting father keep the *Dictionary*. Therefore, as father said, 'the dictionary belongs to me' and he had paid £890 for it in total.

Thus, Tommy's repeated claims that the *Dictionary* belonged to *him* were untrue.

Honour thy father and thy mother

Towards the end of 1994 I travelled from Japan to visit our parents in London and recorded in my diary the following account of Tommy's behaviour (22 December):

> There was a most unfortunate incident with Tom. He had turned up and was in the kitchen. I thought I would talk to him but he was, as usual, in a grumpy mood. He was stuffing his face with food which D had provided, and then started complaining about the mince pies, two sorts of which had been set before him, referring to the home-made ones as 'fucking awful'. He said he didn't see any point in pleasantries; he wanted to complain about my bad behaviour, and he had a long list. Then he started raving—literally raving—about how unfriendly I had been when he visited us in Tokyo in 1988, and other imagined wrongs. It was so unpleasant the only thing I could do was to walk out.

Later I sent him a letter about this incident:

> I was sorry that we missed the opportunity of having a proper talk when I was in London. Your extraordinary outburst made communication impossible. I do not understand what you were trying to achieve, but it saddened me to see your face contorted with rage. I can only interpret such behaviour

as meaning that you wish to be completely estranged from me, and if that is so it will be easy to achieve.

It seems you have a long list of grievances about me. What I find remarkable is the fact that you seem eaten up with anger by what happened, or you imagine happened, five, ten, even forty years ago. It seems your anger has no end; it does you no good, being talked about *ad nauseam* and boiling inside you. What a pity you can't use this energy in a constructive way. There is no sense from you of trying to heal the breach between us, such as it might be. Your list of real or imagined grievances is absurd—but the remarkable thing is that it seems you will never get over them! You are still hanging on to these problems—which are like a millstone around your neck—for *decades*. This is disturbed behaviour. It never seems to occur to you that maybe you were wrong. You seem totally to lack insight. The point, however, is not who was right and who was wrong, but why are you in such a rage? It seems to stem from some kind of envy towards me—God knows why. The problem comes from within you, not from me, or from D or anyone else. The longer you live the more experiences you accumulate—good and bad—and you have to learn to integrate them, to accept them, to take the rough with the smooth. Of course if you give a one-sided view of any particular incident you can get someone to agree with your version of events, but what is the point? So that you can feel justified in your all-consuming anger towards your own brother?

I too could give a long list of things I object to about your behaviour, but I won't, except to point out what I feel is a real cause of a breach between us, and that is the way you abuse our parents.

This concerns, first, your incessant whining to them, and especially to D, about every minor development of your every problem. How can a woman take seriously a middle-aged man who has to tell every detail of his personal and even intimate life to his 80 year old father? It is not as if you are asking for advice; you don't want to hear the sensible advice which D often gives you. You seem just to want to complain, reducing him and M to a state of exasperation. This is not merely a sign of immaturity: it is infantilism.

Second, I object to your appallingly bad manners towards our parents. The way you complained about the mince pies in such an offensive manner when I was there was horrible.

Finally, there is self-absorption about you or egocentricity which somehow seems to prevent you being genuinely interested in anyone else, except in so far as they may be of use to you. For example, when M was in the hospital with a broken leg [this happened earlier in the year], it seems you couldn't have cared less, but found it rather inconvenient that she was out when you called! No doubt this is tied up with your other problems. If you think I am exaggerating, ask yourself why you are so unhappy most of the time!

A similar incident which I also recorded occurred on 19 July 1999 when I was again visiting our parents:

> Went to the local branch of HSBC and D came with me for the walk. On the way back we did some window shopping and by the time we got home were somewhat tired and hungry. D had just sat down to lunch when the bell rang and Tom let himself in with his key. I greeted him in a friendly manner and invited him on our parents' behalf to sit down and join us at lunch. Then I tried to shake his hand but he snatched his hand from mine saying he wanted to talk to father. I said D had just come in and was tired, but T responded angrily that I shouldn't tell him what to do. Mummy was annoyed and said, 'You've got a face like death.' He did indeed look grim and desperate. His response—outside the door—was to call her a 'bitch'. I restrained myself from any action, and shortly after he left. I am not sure if this was because D—for once!—told him off and asked him to leave. Their usual attitude was

'it doesn't matter', or 'one shouldn't say anything' for fear of making it worse.

When I had returned to Japan I wrote to Tommy about this deplorable behaviour:

> I have to say that I found you behaviour at lunch-time a week ago, to put it mildly, regrettable. I don't mean your offensive behaviour to me, for I am past being offended by anything you do or say to me, but I refer to your shocking attitude and words to M & D. You turned up unannounced and uninvited as you frequently do. Does it ever occur to you that this is discourteous and selfish? You came on that day for you own purposes without any regard for the convenience of those on whom you called, expecting, or rather demanding, immediate attention. When I pointed out to you that Daddy has just come in from a long walk and was tired and had just sat down to lunch, you rudely told me to mind my own business. Although I rose to shake your hand and welcome you to join us for lunch, when you could have responded in kind, you even withdrew your hand from my grasp in your impatience and irritability. Mummy's comment that you 'looked like death' I thought only too true. What one could regard as unforgivable, however, was your response to this, which was to call your own mother a 'bitch'.

Another illustration of his attitude problem occurred after I had immigrated to Japan. I had met a splendidly eccentric Englishman, Anthony Willoughby, who ran courses at the Great Wall of China for business people to inspire them to fulfil their potential and 'achieve success for themselves and their organization.' The name of the company was 'I will not complain' (*sic*). Once I bought Tommy as a present a T-shirt with the name of this organisation emblazoned on the front. Did it raise a smile in him? No, he complained all the more. For him, complaining is a way of life.

Grand country living

An egregious example of Tommy's unrealistic and dependent behaviour was conveyed to me in a letter from father of 4 August 1998:

> After spending a lot of money to improve the little house in Narcissus Road [in West Hampstead to which he had then recently moved] he saw an advertisement in *Country Life* for a house for sale in Chippenham, about ten miles from Bath. He went to see it and fell in love with it. To quote from the brochure: 'An important part of a magnificent Grade I listed Baroque mansion.' It has five bedrooms and three bathrooms and a private garden. The price: £405,000, of which he will have to put down 10 per cent, £40,500 (non-returnable). Will Renata lend this to him? He'll pay it back in six months, he says. He won't be able to. Of course he will have to sell his house in Narcissus Road; it appears an estate agent has found a buyer but estate agents don't work for nothing. T will have to give him his cut, and that is only the beginning of T's expenses in quitting Narcissus Road and hurrying off to Chippenham. There is stamp duty to pay and the cost of removing all his furniture and books—that will be several thousand pounds.
>
> He won't stay in Chippenham; he'll be lonely there. Liam, who is wedded to his computer, will have no time for him and T has anyhow to be in London to see his son Toby and attend auction sales. When in London he'll want to stay at No 81 with us. And pay a gardener for the enclosed garden of the house in Chippenham.
>
> T dismisses all my arguments. He already owes me £18,742 for various bills of his which I paid, Toby's school fees, etc., and £9,500 for T to pay Christie's in New York.
>
> Finally, there will come a time when my plays will be performed and they will earn a great deal of money. In my present frame of mind I want to go to Sullivan [a respected local solicitor] who drew up my will to get him to change it,

and cut T out. But another mood may overcome my bitterness and I'll probably not cut T out.

I saw the advertisement myself since I subscribed to *Country Life* for my waiting room. It was indeed an impressive residence. But for Tommy to make such a move would likely have put him under financial strain. And as noted it would have meant him living with our elderly parents for days at a time when he was in London. Even in their ever-indulgent attitude they would have balked at that!

In spite of this, mother at first allowed herself to be persuaded to lend, that is, give, Tommy £40,500—a considerable portion of her nest egg for emergencies in her and father's old age. But she wasn't happy about it. She discussed this matter with me on the phone and as a result changed her mind. Tommy was irate. It didn't end there, of course. He continued to nag our parents for money so he could press ahead with his unrealistic house moving plan.

Having been drawn into this absurd situation I found it necessary to send Tommy a fax on 24 August 1998:

> I should remind you that No 81 is actually my property and M & D are living there at my invitation. Without my consent you have no right to stay there, and in any case they do not wish to have you as a lodger on your visits to London if you decide to live in the country. I suppose it has never occurred to you that you should refer to me if you had such an idea!
>
> In addition, you seem unaware, or you do not care, that for the past month you have caused our aged parents considerable distress with your constant nagging about moving to Chippenham. It is a great shame that on Mummy's 85th birthday, of all times, you caused her particular agitation by expressing your anger over her change of heart about lending you money. If you had any respect for our parents you would never have asked them for money in the first place. In any case, I understand that you already owe D around £39,000

which he was misguided enough to lend you to pay for Toby's school fees.

As I have mentioned before, your dependency on our aged parents is abnormal. They cannot have many more years left in this life and you should treat them with more consideration. If you want to move to the country and can afford it, do so, but I ask you not to involve M & D in this and in every personal and even intimate matter of your life. It is wrong for you to use them as a cheap line of credit, lodging house, free restaurant, etc.

I might have saved myself the bother.

Olive branch
Nonetheless, a short-lived kind of truce did occur towards the end of 1999. There was a letter from Tommy in which he said we should end the feud between us and try to get on better together. This was very welcome!

On 19 December 1999 I recorded the following entry in my diary:

> Went to dinner with Tommy this evening. Quite difficult at first, with him saying he wasn't hungry since he'd had a large lunch. It was at a restaurant called The Vale in Maida Vale, which at least had the attraction of being non-smoking, though the food wasn't all that good. Tommy didn't eat anything except a morsel from my plate and a desert, but we shared a bottle of wine. He spent a long time telling me about his medical problems, especially a burning sensation in his right hand, arm and leg, and across his face, with a bilateral headache. These symptoms came on immediately after a diagnostic lumbar sympathetic block which he had had done to investigate his chronic testicular pain. I felt he shouldn't have subjected himself to this, but he didn't ask my opinion in advance. I could only say that there was no serious reason why the procedure should have had such an effect

and I thought it would cease sooner or later, which greatly cheered him.

Alas, this brief warming of the relationship between Tommy and me didn't last long.

The birthday parties
Our parents were close in age, mother being seven months older than father. When mother reached the venerable age of 90 I thought it would be nice to arrange a special birthday celebration: we could have a lunch for family and friends, perhaps at Kenwood House or at a five-star hotel. Being so far away, in Japan, I asked Tommy, since he lived in London, to help with the arrangements, in particular by visiting one or two venues to see if they were suitable. Would he do this? No. He claimed to be too busy but I suspect the real reason was he did not want to cooperate with me as a matter of principle, and of course he would not offer to contribute to the cost. So I had to do all the work myself. But I had written to him on 4 July 2003:

> As of course you know, it will be Mummy's 90th birthday on 7 August, and I am sure that the nicest birthday present we could give her would be for us to be friends again! Don't you agree?
> Mummy has told me that she mentioned to you already the idea I had for a birthday celebration, but apparently you are not very enthusiastic; this is a great pity.
> I had hoped we could organise a birthday lunch at a good restaurant, taking a private room, and assisting her to invite any guests that she wishes. For example, Mrs— needs to come in a wheelchair, so a suitable taxi or minivan would have to be booked for this. I have heard that there are private rooms at Kenwood House. Clearly I need your help in setting this up since I am so far away. We can share the cost. I plan to visit England in sufficient time for this event, arriving August 6th and leaving on 9th.

Let us put aside our differences (such as they may be) and co-operate for this unique and wonderful occasion. I will call you soon to discuss this further, or you can of course call me.

This appeal went unheeded so I wrote to him again on 22 July 2003:

I had hoped—in vain!—that you would cooperate with me for Mummy's 90th birthday. Your admitted lack of enthusiasm when we spoke on the phone this morning together with your annoyance over my objections to inviting your old girlfriend, Mairead, are difficult to understand. This is supposed to be a birthday celebration for Mummy, not a party for your ex-girlfriend.

However, all this is beside the point. I am very much disappointed that you cannot put aside your resentments, which go back decades, even for the short time between now and 7 August. Obviously, I need you to look at two or three potential venues. Couldn't you have gone into Claridges and checked out the private dining room? For me to come to England requires considerable organisation which I cannot leave till the last minute. For you, a morning spent visiting two or three restaurants in the West End to discuss costs, etc., and get back to me, would have the whole thing settled. But no. You seem to live entirely wrapped up in yourself; even Mummy's 90th birthday makes no difference to your selfishness. No wonder you are so unhappy!

Thus I had to arrange and pay for everything myself, though with the internet it wasn't too difficult, and I organised a private luncheon party at The Dorchester near Hyde Park. It was a splendid affair. As well as our parents and some of their friends, Tommy came together with his son, Toby, and his son's mother, Maureen; he also brought along his business partner, Liam.

Father's 90th birthday occurred in March the following year, 2004. By this time, because of additional unresolved problems with Tommy, our relationship had gone from bad to worse. Once again, I made the arrangements myself for a luncheon celebration, this time at the Berkeley Hotel, but prior to that (8 March 2004) I sent the following fax to Tommy:

> Because of your behaviour over the parking fine [described below] you have caused a lot of trouble to my tenants, the letting agents, and me, to say nothing of the trouble to yourself.
> When I called to try to confirm that you had sorted the matter out, instead of apologising, you were evasive and argumentative. It seems your absurd and never-ending resentment, which is festering away under the surface, boils over at the slightest provocation, and you become enraged and abusive.
> I think such behaviour is a sign not just of a psychological disturbance, but actually mad.
> Obviously, you will not now wish to partake of my hospitality and therefore will not be attending the lunch at the Berkeley Hotel. If Toby and Maureen wish to come they are welcome.

The lunch was a great success. But no one from Tommy's side showed up, which was a pity.

6

BLAMING OTHERS

WHEN OUR FATHER died Tommy gave me only *three days notice* to arrange to travel from Japan to attend his funeral. Obviously, this was impossible. Then I was roundly criticised and my omission broadcast to anyone who would listen, as reported to me in these words: 'Can you imagine, can you imagine? Gabriel didn't even attend his father's funeral!' The tragic situation around our parent's deaths is fully described later.

Similarly, when our mother died it was shortly before my daughter's school-leaving celebrations at The King's School, Canterbury. Tommy found out by phoning my wife on which day this event was due to take place. It appears he did this, not in order to avoid arranging our mother's funeral on a day which would clash with an important arrangement I would not want to miss, but because it *would* clash. Doubtless he complained ever after about my non-attendance at this funeral too.

Yet another example was from the time when Tommy made his one and only visit to Japan to see me and my family. Or rather, he came not so much to see us, but for business reasons: he was hoping to establish contact with Japanese booksellers and develop this market.

My wife made of a point of never calling me at work unless it was an emergency. This happened only twice. Once was when our younger son locked himself in the bathroom and was in a panic. There wasn't anything I could do but fortunately a helpful workman who happened to be in the garden below had a ladder by which he was able to enter through the window and rescue the little lad. The second time was in connection with Tommy's visit. In Japan, as is well known, you must take off your shoes when you enter someone's home. Japanese homes are built to facilitate this transition: the front door of apartments and houses always opens outwards and there is an area just inside the entrance, the *genkan,* where you remove your shoes and then take a small step up onto the floor level of the dwelling. Usually guest slippers are provided. The invitation to enter one's home in Japanese is *Oagari kudasai*—please come up.

To fail to take off your shoes in this situation is the height of bad manners. Tommy had only been with us one day and he probably merely forgot, but when this omission was pointed out to him, instead of apologising, he argued and was quite unpleasant to my wife. She called me in exasperation to say she couldn't stand having him as a guest, though she later relented. He also expected her to run around for him as a guide and interpreter—something she wasn't able to do since she was in early pregnancy and feeling unwell. Subsequently, Tommy criticised me to anyone who would listen, for my terrible lack of hospitality!

Wicked uncle

Another example of an unfortunate characteristic of Tommy's behaviour is that he would, apparently deliberately, set up a situation from which unhappy consequences followed, for which he would then blame *other people*, especially me.

Tommy's son, Toby, had an open invitation to visit my family in Tokyo, but this was never taken up. Once, when he was a small boy I sent him a birthday present—a figurine of fierce-looking Samurai warrior. Tommy took objection to this for some reason and was critical of it. Years later he added to his long list of complaints about me the fact that I never sent Toby birthday cards. Then why didn't he tell me about this omission at the time and provide me with his address? The reason is that he deliberately created a distance between us—and then blamed me for it. And I don't recall that Tommy ever sent birthday cards to my children.

Now Toby, who as far as I could see grew up to be a fine young man, started life under less than ideal circumstances.

He was raised by a single parent, his mother, Maureen. Tommy was undoubtedly fond of his son but they never lived together. Sometimes when both Toby's parents met, from what I heard they had violent quarrels. And since I had been deliberately excluded from involvement with Toby I only met him on rare occasions on my visits to London.

In an email from Tommy which I deal with in Chapter 10, among much else I was informed that 'Toby needed psychoanalysis because of his wicked uncle.' This is not satire—Tommy has no sense of humour over this sort of thing—so what does it mean? In the context of the email as a whole, it's just an insult.

***

Of the many complaints Tommy had and still has against me, one in particular requires elaboration.

I moved to Japan in 1984 and for the first few years worked as a salaried assistant at a clinic serving the foreign population of Tokyo. In 1992 I was able to set up my own independent clinic, the Tokyo British Clinic. While I was employed I took one holiday a year to return to London with my family, which by 1987 consisted of my wife, two children, and me. Our parents rented a charming thatched cottage in the countryside near Banbury in Oxfordshire, and we travelled there by car from London to spend a week in this pleasant place. The cottage had four bedrooms and with four adults and two children the place was full up. Not having seen my parents for a year (they might have made a visit to Tokyo in the meantime) I was looking forward to spending time with just them and my family; I didn't want Tommy muscling in to be there in the cottage as well.

The reason for this was that he wasn't interested in me or my family; he wanted to be with our parents even over this short period to bask in the warm glow of their attention and sympathy for his endless problems! It would not, therefore, be a pleasure to see him. In any case there was no room for extra people—they would have had to sleep on the floor in the living room.

It is now over thirty years ago, so my memory of the details is a little hazy. As I recall, we had been in the cottage for a day or two when father received a phone call from Tommy: he was on his way to join us with his infant son. He had invited himself at very short notice, and father didn't have the presence of mind to say it was unsuitable due to insufficient accommodation, or at least to confer with me first. Two or three hours later Tommy turns up in his car with Toby. I believe Maureen was with them but Tommy disputes this. I objected to him imposing himself on our family gathering and asked him to leave. He did so, taking Toby and Maureen (if she was there) with him and, as he later told me, they arrived back in London at midnight. This is odd because Banbury is no more than a two hours' drive from London and he left in the afternoon, not late in the evening. But Tommy has never been able to forget, much less to forgive me, for this incident.

If it was as Tommy claimed, that father had indeed invited them, and as I and my family were his and mother's guests, it is barely believable that he did not assert himself and tell me that Tommy and Toby (and Maureen if she came too) were joining us. And why did father not ask me in advance of Tommy setting out if I was happy to have in our family gathering? What is clear is that Tommy, with our without Toby and Maureen, could meet our parents at any time. Why did he have to come during the brief period when we were visiting from Japan? In any case, with his grumpy face and surly manner it was no pleasure to see him; if he had stayed it would have ruined the holiday for me. It seemed to me that he didn't care about this, but was jealous that I should spend even a week with our parents without him. Anybody else would have conferred with me and considered whether it was reasonable to impose himself on our busy parents who were catering for six people in a cottage that was already full to the rafters.

Holes in the stair carpet
In order to understand Tommy's outburst in his 2005 email which will be revealed shortly, it is necessary to know more about the situation at No 81. When I acquired this flat in 1975 it was unmodernised but I gradually had it improved: new kitchen and bathroom, central heating, double glazing, redecorated throughout, and fitted carpets on the stairs and in the bedrooms. But carpets tend to wear out, and the stair carpet in particular, being subject to the most wear, eventually developed two or three holes. This was dangerous: someone might catch their foot in one of the holes and take a tumble, and I therefore wanted to have the stair carpet replaced. But as it was a long time since I had had redecoration carried out I thought it would make better sense to have the whole flat redecorated before replacing the stair carpet. However, our parents, who at that time had been living there for about ten years, didn't want the upheaval that this would entail, so I agreed to replace the carpet only. Of course they could, and perhaps should, have organised this themselves. But to save them the bother I arranged and paid for a high quality new stair carpet to be laid down, the colour being of their choosing.

Fridge fracas
A related matter concerned the fitted fridge in the kitchen of my flat. Having been installed some twenty years previously it was not surprising that one day it ceased to function and needed to be replaced. Well, as it was *my* flat, *I* wanted to arrange this. Simple? Not where Tommy was concerned. But why was he involved at all? The reason was that as our parents aged they became more and more involved with and dependent upon him; their household became a veritable *ménage à trois*. Thus, when a new fridge was needed and I intended to ask a firm I knew to oversee the work, I came up against a difficulty: Tommy. He had already arranged for a workman friend of his to install a new fridge on the cheap, but mother did not want to tell me about this for fear of 'upsetting' me! Then I wrote to mother on 18 November 2003 as follows:

Allow me to point out that your desire not to upset me is upsetting! If you simply would say, 'Tommy is dealing with the kitchen, there is no need for you to bother,' that would be fine, and it would save me the trouble. I simply wished to help you have the improvements you needed in the kitchen carried out in the most efficient way. The real reason for your hesitation is now clear. Since T involved himself in having a new fridge fitted in my kitchen without telling me, you apparently don't want to upset *him* by telling him that *I* will do it. Why ever not? Why can't you straightforwardly say to him that I'm dealing with the matter, so he can forget about it? After all, it is my flat and my kitchen! Why do you have to treat T with kid gloves all the time? The fact that you are afraid to upset him implies that he might, indeed, be upset. But he is a man in late middle age, not a small child!

Window stuck open and ceiling falling down
The terrace of which No 81 is a part was probably built around the middle of the nineteenth century. Old houses need maintenance. In the early 2000s two structural problems developed which required urgent attention. The upper half of the sash window in the bathroom became stuck in the open position and it was only the secondary (double) glazing that kept the elements out. Then, in the living room, or drawing room as father called it, which was also used by mother as a consulting room for her clients, a substantial piece of the decorative moulding of the ceiling had fallen down; if it was not repaired there was a danger of more pieces of the ceiling coming away. The obvious thing to do, therefore, was to contact a builder to have these repairs carried out. I could hardly organise this from Japan, so Tommy should have helped. But would he? No. He refused to do anything about these problems and then *blamed me* for letting the flat fall into disrepair! In the meantime, it wasn't very pleasant for our parents to live in my flat which was unsafe through deliberate neglect by Tommy.

No 12 and the parking fine
It was not only the situation at No 81 which gave rise to the charming email we shall come to soon. An absurd—almost mad—state of affairs arose in connection with the ownership of my flat at 12 Belsize Court (No 12). The matter is complicated and I ask for the reader's patience while I explain it.

John Symonds was a writer of novels, children's books, biographies, and plays. One of his most successful works was the biography of a character called Aleister Crowley, the self-styled wickedest man in the world, who set up a pseudo-religion involving sex, drugs, and black magic. John's definitive biography of him ran to three editions, the last of which, published in 1997, was called *The Beast 666*. Now, according to Crowley's will which was supposed to come into effect at his death in 1947, John was made his literary executor, and on this basis and in good faith he used material from Crowley's *oeuvre* to write his biography.

There was just one problem: Crowley was an undischarged bankrupt and therefore his will was invalid. John's scholarly work about Crowley, it has to be said, is written in a mildly satirical fashion and this displeased the 'true believers' in Crowleyanity who belonged to an organisation in America called the Ordo Templi Orientis. They showed their displeasure by having someone attempt to set fire to the publisher's warehouse where copies of *Beast* were stored, though the would-be arsonist was apprehended by the police, and by two men physically attacking John at the door of his home. But father was no feeble old man; he fought them off and they fled. These illegal methods having failed to subdue John, they next brought a lawsuit in the High Court in London for breach of copyright. The case was eventually decided in favour of the plaintiffs on a technicality, and John had to pay substantial, though not ruinous, damages.

While the case was dragging its way through the Court, there was concern among John's legal advisors that if he lost, the damages might be beyond his means, and therefore he was advised to reduce his assets if it could legally be done.

Our parents at this time were living in my flat (No 81) which I had vacated on moving to Japan. They had another flat, 12 Belsize Court (No 12) where they never lived but used as a storeroom for their books and occasionally to put people up. It was stated in our parents' wills of 2000 that No 12 was to be left to me when they died. I had no wish to acquire it earlier and indeed suggested they should redecorate the place and let it so that *they* could enjoy the rental income, but they did not want to do this. Now, because of the lawsuit, it was arranged that I should acquire No 12 from my parents in their lifetime by a simple legal deed. This was achieved with the assistance of the family accountant, Clive Burnett, and title to the property was transferred to me in 2003. Also, father made me a loan of £100,000 which it was agreed I would return in due course. By these means our parents' assets were reduced, but as it turned out such precautions were unnecessary. When the case was over I repaid the loan plus interest.

Although I was grateful to Burnett for his work in connection with transferring No 12 to my name and for his assistance with father's lawsuit, he turned out to be a snake in the grass, as will be explained later.

It will be remembered that Tommy had already been given a comparable flat, No 66, which, because of his foolish behaviour he had to sell at a knock-down price.

I now come to the matter of the parking fine. For a number of years after our parents acquired No 12, Tommy—I am not sure whether it was with or without their knowledge and consent—falsely gave that address as the place where he kept his car. This was a criminal offence. The actual place he kept it was outside his home, about one mile away. And why did he do that? It was to *evade paying parking fines!* He thought the registered address where he allegedly kept his car could not be traced to him if he was given a parking ticket.

When I took over ownership of the property I had it redecorated and then rented it out using a local agent by the name of Kernahans. At that time I had no idea of Tommy's illegal use of the address and he never mentioned it to me. The first I heard of the matter was through an urgent message from Kernahans: my tenants are being harassed by letters from bailiffs, followed by visits from the bailiffs themselves demanding payment for a parking fine imposed on a Mr Thomas J Symonds whose address is given as—12 Belsize Court! In spite of the tenants protesting that they have never heard of Mr Thomas J Symonds, he certainly doesn't live at their address, and they know nothing about the matter, the bailiffs, perhaps not possessing the highest levels of intelligence, or perhaps because they blindly have to follow a protocol, persist to the point of causing serious annoyance and even a feeling of persecution to my tenants. This got so bad that they eventually moved out—and I lost six weeks' rent before the wretched business was cleared up and another tenant found.

As a result of messages from Kernahans and a number of fruitless attempts to get Tommy to deal with the matter, I sent him this fax on 19 March 2004:

> It is most annoying that I have received further communications from Camden Council, via Kernahans, about your dishonest behaviour over unpaid parking fines and giving a false address. In addition, I am told this could involve more inconvenience to my tenants, since the enforcement agencies apparently may still turn up at my flat even though they have been told you don't live there. While I do not wish to cause you trouble, I must warn you that this is the last chance I shall give you before divulging your address to the council. You must immediately pay all outstanding fines and give them your correct address.

Still he did nothing. Months went by and the fine went up. Eventually, I passed on his real address, not to Camden

Council, but to my agent, Kernahans. The next stage in this unedifying story was a message from Kernahans on 25 August 2004:

> Attached scan of a Bailiff Removal Notice [Plate 3] collected from the property today. I will send this on to your brother and will be writing to the Bailiffs advising them of the tenancy details & your brother's address, copies of which will follow. Perhaps in the meantime would you please ask you brother to deal with this urgently?

In the end he had to pay the fine, which by then had gone up to £500, but he used this matter to berate our parents over *my* unreasonable behaviour! They were unable to stand up to him and this fiasco was often mentioned by our mother in a way that was critical of me when we spoke on the phone. She took Tommy's side to complain that I was unreasonable in divulging his real address! It was unfortunate that she allowed herself to be involved at all in this matter. Thus on 21 September 2004 I wrote to her as follows:

> It is most regrettable that when I ring you up to congratulate you on the splendid portrait [see below], and to have a chat about other interesting family matters, you take the opportunity to upset me by mentioning yet again this wretched business of T attempting to evade paying parking fines. As I have pointed out to him, giving a false address to the vehicle licensing authority could result in a *criminal* prosecution for which there could be a heavy fine and the possibility of a *prison sentence*. I have bent over backwards to avoid causing problems for him, but I have no alternative when, in spite of repeated warnings from me, he persists in using my address and the bailiffs are literally knocking on the door of No 12 and causing distress to my tenants. As I mentioned, I merely passed on T's address to Kernahans, as they requested. What else am I supposed to do?

I beg you not to mention this matter again. With respect, it is no concern of yours. Can't you just tell T that and *refuse to be involved?*

Incidentally, I think it is highly irresponsible for T to run up parking fines—and they seem to increase by the week if you don't pay them—to the tune of hundreds of pounds when he is heavily in debt to you and no doubt to other people as well.

Misuse of storage area at No 12

When our parents acquired No 12 there was a communal storage area in which, withpermission, Tommy stored some of father's remaindered books and other books. Then I received on 15 January 2006 the following message from Kernahans:

> Can you help?
>
> I think your brother asked me to store some of your father's books in the storage area in the north boiler house. There are a substantial number of boxes of books in this area taking up about 40 per cent of the storage of this building.
>
> I have been asked to evaluate the storage area and open it up for all residents and I would appreciate, given the fact that your brother has had the facility to store the books for a number of years now, if he could have them removed within seven days.
>
> I would appreciate it if you counld point me in the right direction or make contact to assist us.

On receipt of this message I wrote to Tommy asking him to sort this matter out. So what does Tommy do? He removes the boxes and dumps them in the communal entrance hall of my flat at No 81! They were piled up high and causing inconvenience to the tenants on the ground floor. Therefore I had to send another fax, on 21 January 2006:

Although most of the books belong to M & D, you effectively abandoned them several years ago when you put them in the storeroom at Belsize Court, and it is therefore up to you to dispose of them responsibly when asked to do so. This does not mean dumping them at No 81 and cluttering up the common entrance hall. (There is no space to put them in the flat.)

You seem to have the curious idea that because our parents live in my flat, this gives you some kind of right to make use of the premises for your own purposes. You have neither right to use the flat nor the entrance hall at No 81 in any way whatsoever and I expressly forbid you to do so.

So then what does Tommy do? It is reflected in yet another fax I had to send him, on 31 January 2006:

> I told you I did not want those unwanted books from No 12 put in my flat at No 81. Yet you deliberately and against my express wish did just that. Then I heard you have moved all the boxes from the downstairs hall into the flat and have distributed them around all the rooms including the attic. You have no right to do this and I insist you remove all the all boxes immediately.

My parents at that time were nonagenarians and couldn't stand up to Tommy—but then they hardly ever did throughout their lives.

> Saturday 15 November '86
>
> Tommy: He would drive you potty, as he almost drives me. He easily succumbs to tears, and is full of regrets about pretty well everything. That on the one hand. On the other he is stubborn to the point of perversity. It is not that he hasn't the brains or the energy to do this or that that he should do, must do, it is that he won't – just to be bloody minded. Hence his stomach pains. I've told him a thousand times to give up taking tablets and running to doctors for only he can cure himself by one of two methods or by both: enduring the conflict and waiting to see what will co(em) out of it, not prolonging the conflict by failing to face it; that extends the neurosis. And two by doing the things, such as paying his bills, which he knows he ought to do, but won't. If he did this, he'd shed his resentment. He collapses into babyhood, to which I said, 'Well, that's all right as long as you know what you are doing.'
>
> Because of the turmoil he has been in, he has, I believe, learnt a lot (which he won't admit of course) and is in some ways already a nicer person. The problem is, I think, to free himself from the childhood psyche; there is a greater personality waiting in the wings to emerge. But meanwhile, oh, dear, oh, dear, he goes on and on. For the last few nights he has slept here and in the morning he greets me with the remark that he is as bad as ever. It is not true and he has admitted that, suddenly and for no reason, his pains have gone, but they come back. His so-called pains are his reason for remaining stuck. That is why I don't believe in his pains no matter what he says.
>
> I've written this about T because you are concerned and I want to put you in the picture to the best of my ability.
>
> love
> D

Plate 1. Part of a letter from John Symonds to the author about Tommy's behaviour.

Tom owes me £530
£780 ÷ 2 = £ 390 + 110 rebinding = £500
Therefore Tom owes me £30,
which sum he paid 10 Jan 80
we are now quits and the
dictionary belongs to me

Plate 2. Extract from a page of one of John Symonds's account books explaining how he is the owner of the Johnson *Dictionary* (re-written below for clarity).

EQUITA BAILIFFS

YOUR DETAILS:
Thomas J Symonds
Flat 12 Belsize Court
Wedderburn Road
LONDON
NW3 5QJ

OUR REF	8546961
CLIENT REF	CD71058671
DATE	06/08/2004

BAILIFF REMOVAL

We are to attend your property shortly to remove goods in connection to your unpaid Penalty Charge Notice debt due to London Borough Of Camden.

We will be in your area throughout the coming week and will enforce the warrant without any further notice, which includes removing goods (including motor vehicles), even if you are not in attendance.

To avoid this action you must contact us immediately 0870 5581581 and make immediate arrangements to pay this debt now

Winston Mitchell

Winston Mitchell
Head of Removals

MUST PAY:
£365.56

Equita Ltd 42-44 Henry Street, Northampton NN1 4BZ Tel: 01604 628360
Registered in England: 3168371 Registered Office: 42-44 Henry Street, Northampton, NN1 4BZ Vat No 618 1841 40

Plate 3. Bailiff Removal Notice showing the false address Mr Thomas J Symonds used for where he kept his car—a criminal offence.

```
              TOKYO BRITISH CLINIC
              DAIKANYAMA Y BUILDING 2F
              2-13-7 EBISU-NISHI, SHIBUYA-KU
              TOKYO 150-0021, JAPAN
              e-mail: gsymonds@gol.com
              Tel: +81 3 5458 6099
              Fax: +81 3 5458-6095
```

TO   : Mr Thomas J Symonds

FAX NO : 0063-44-20-7435-1299

FROM   : Dr G Symonds

DATE   : 21 July 2005

PAGE(S) : 1 inclusive

Your rudeness to me and your selfishness are of an extreme degree. I am afraid this behaviour shows you must be actually mad or, to put it more charitably, you are pitiable.

As I have already told you, this is a family emergency. Don't you understand this?

I hope that when you are old — you are already quite old — and if you are in trouble, your son will not treat you as you treat your parents.

I must repeat — unless you wish our father to die — the only sensible thing is for you to take him to stay with you in your house. I will take care of all your out-of-pocket expenses.

I beg you to put aside your resentment, try to break out of your self absorption, and give this matter you top priority.

G.

Return the £500 you stole from me & the Dictionary.

Plate 4. The author's fax returned with Tommy's scribbled demands at the bottom.

Plate 5. John and Renata Symonds's Woolwich Guernsey statement showing balance on 23 April 2003.

Pindar Press
Publishers
40 Narcissus Road. London NW6 1TH
Tel: 020 7435 2629
Fax 020 7435 1288
e-mail: editor@pindarpress.co.uk

28 April 2005

1. Most importantly of all. DON'T LET HIM BULLY YOU. YOU DO WHAT YOU WANT.

2. You don't want a stairlift-too expensive father would never use it etc.etc.

3. You want to move to 12 Belsize court to be on one floor and a place that is modernized.

4 81 is falling to bits and he as the landlord should get the windows repaired in the front bedroom and bathroom. The windows are permanently open and need to be shut and opened when you want. The shower is broken and is not working properly. The bath leaks -taps leak and need replacing. The whole ceiling in the sitting room is in danger of falling down and needs urgent attention.

5. Don't let him throw anything away whithout yoour permission.

6. Don't let him remove anything from the house like pictures on walls, books etc.

7. Don't let him throw away your books from 12 Belsize Court which I brought round and he threatened to have removed.

8. To summarize that is your flat in the sense you are sitting tenants and he has no right to even be in the flat -only with your agreement but nothing else- Remember that.

9. He only wnats to get rid of your money so there is nothing for me. He is all right because you have already given him 12 Belsize court.

10 You are probably moving to Winchester Rd so you can escape the clutches of Gabriel.

11 Under no circumstances should you give Gabriel power of attorney.

Plate 6. Tommy's instructions to our mother with list of warnings about the author.

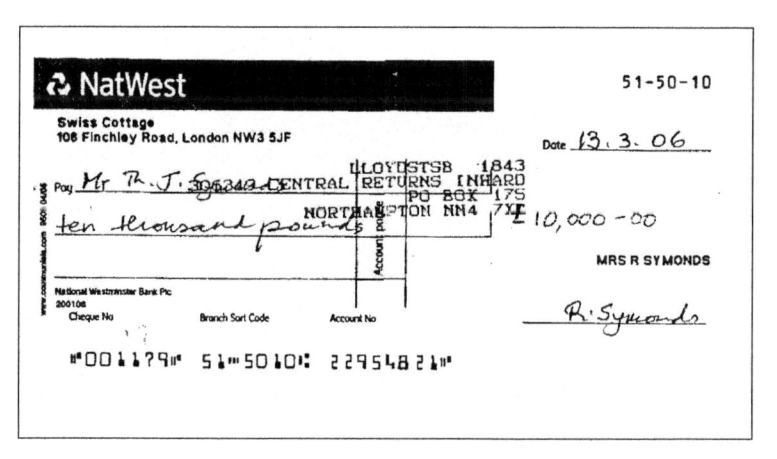

Plate 7. Cheque in favour of Mr Th. J. Symonds for £10,000 drawn by Renata Symonds.

Plate 8. Credit slip from NatWest cheque book showing that Renata Symonds's account was converted to a joint account with Mr T J Symonds.

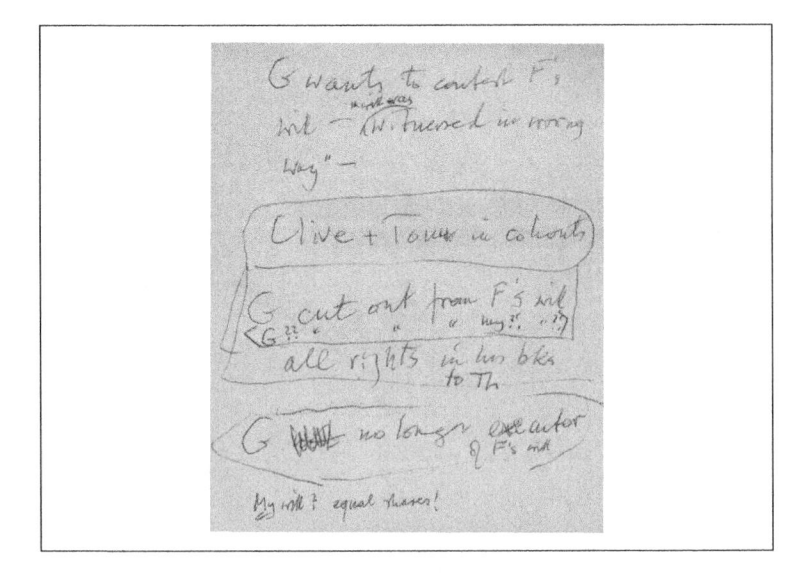

Plate 9. A page from Renata Symonds's note pad which she used to remind herself of important facts, due to her failing memory.

RECEIPT

27.09.2004

Re. Portrait in Oils of Renata Symonds

Received from Gabriel Symonds   £8275.00
(including expenses £275.00)

Michael Taylor
1 upper Street
Child Okeford
Blandford
Dorset DT11 8EF

01258 860232

Michael Jay
Michael Taylor

Plate 10. Receipt from the artist, Michael Taylor, for the portrait of Renata Symonds..

Plate 11. Cover of brochure of the Royal Society of Portrait Painters' annual exhibition, 2005, showing the portrait of Renata Symonds which was later stolen by Tommy.

> **From:** Tom Symonds [tom@pindarpress.co.uk]
> **Sent:** 26 March 2007 21:31
> **To:** gsymonds@gol.com
> **Subject:** Dictionary & Diaries
>
> Return my father's dairies which were left to me in his will and were illegally removed from 81 Belsize Lane without his or my mother's permission and return the Joihnson Dictioany which belonged to me and my father and left to me in his will and I will allow the Geffrye Museum to have the portrait subject to my mother being in agreement. It is that simple.

Plate 12. Blackmail message from Tommy demanding the return of goods he claims belong to him as a condition for releasing the stolen portrait of Renata Symonds to the Jeffrye Museum.

> **From:** Tom Symonds [tom@pindarpress.co.uk]
> **Sent:** 03 July 2007 02:03
> **To:** gsymonds@gol.com
> **Subject:** Contents of 81
>
> Dear Gabriel
>
> You had absolutely no right to remove the contents of 81 for storage without my agreement which I did not grant, if you have done that. Youy have omitted to mention
> mention items such as the book case above father's desk, the fridge the hob the cooker and the washing machine, the book shelves in the top room -these are all mine and under the wills as is everything other than the suite in the sitting room and the glazed book case everything else is mine. If the parents gave me things before they died that is between them and me just as you were given certain things before they died. You have omitted to mention some major items in your list, the windsor chair by the door all mothers books and papers in her bedroom and in the sitting room, runners, carpets, all mother's music , the list is endless, but I know exactly what was there including TV whic has been removed. All these things belong to me. You have tried but failed to get the wills changed because they do not suitand therefore it is not true to say they belong to you as much as to me.
>
> Please tell me where they are being stored.
> I intend to write to you with a bigger list
>
> With best wishes,
>
> Tom Symonds

Plate 13. Email to the author of Tommy's false claims, with cynical 'best wishes'.

From: Tom [mailto:sales@pindarpress.co.uk]
Sent: 22 August 2005 06:55
To: gsymonds@gol.com
Subject: Re: Infantilism

You have kept quiet about my dictionary because you are thoroughly nasty and a cheat .I am not prepared to do any deals with you. If my father told you to keep it this is pure chicanery on your part. You were not born yesterday and you know perfectly well that he is not capable of saying no to you. When my parents transferred £100,000-00 pounds to you when Clive Burnett was afraid that the OTO might get hold of it you steadfastly held on to it for months after my mother had asked you to return it and then in the same dishonest way you said my father said you could keep it knowing full well that he neither meant it nor had the right to give it to you.

You are one of the most evil and nasty people I have ever known or heard about. You have kept Renata as a slave for decades with you bullying nasty ways. You know all this and that she is afraid of you but you can only exist when you control and humiliate people. ▬▬▬▬▬▬▬
▬▬▬▬▬▬ No 12 was put in your name purely because of Clive's fear that the OTO might get their hands on it. After the risk had subsided you should have handed it back but you told my mother that you wanted to let it and refurbish it, as if you needed it for a medical condition. My mother only gave you that flat because she could not say no to you when you said you wanted it.You then proceeded in a scandalous way to chuck away £30000-00 more than you needed, to refurbish it. It should have cost £10000. You are despicable and flash with cash and your nastiness knows no bounds.

When you decided to employ Cerina you did so to only to bully my parents. You never discussed with them whether they were going to pay and they will not.Renata thought you were doing it because you are kind. You are not kind but evil and nasty and even she knows this at last. We did not want to discuss the matter with you because there is never any discussion with you. You are only capable of bullying people and telling them what to do. My parents will not pay for Kerina. Carole whom you tried to throw out because she has a baby in exactly the same way you ejected your own nephew almost 20 years ago, has proved somebody my parents prefer having around their flat and is a lot cheaper. They would never have agreed to Cerina if they had known you would expect them to pay. Yes I have no doubt they will not stand up to you and you will then say they have agreed to pay. Don't you see-dick head, they are afraid of you but they are only agreeing because of the fear.You cannot re-negotiate a deal after the event. We will pay this time for this so keep your ugly proboscis out of our affairs.
When I tell people of what you did to Toby and how you have neglected him all these years they do not believe me and they think I am joking. You say you hope Toby does not treat me the way I treat my parents. You are sick.▬▬▬▬▬▬▬▬▬▬▬▬▬▬▬▬
▬▬▬▬▬▬▬▬▬▬▬▬▬▬▬▬▬▬▬▬▬▬▬▬▬▬▬▬▬▬▬▬▬
▬▬▬▬▬▬▬▬▬▬▬▬▬ Everybody who comes into contact with you hates and despises you. For you to have refused Toby to stay the night-I had to take him back to London at midnight-Outrageous. Renata should have told you to fuck off back to Japan there and then. She wasn't even living at 81 at the time and was paying for Long cottage. The reason you tell me your tenants left is because they don't want a shit for a landlord. No body leaves because a bailiff calls when your tenants were at work and some baillifs letters are sent. I had been using the address of number 12 for many years before you got your hands on it by chicanery and there was never a problem. Return my dictionary and the £500 you stole from me. You and Masumi treated me worse that a dog when I visited you in Japan and you have never apologised for that or the time you ejected me from 81.I might as well say you owe me £20000-00 for all the mental stress you have caused in the family, and the analysis Toby needed because of his wicked Uncle. There is more sense in that. One of your problems is that you are incapable of admitting a fault. When ever Renata hints at something you don't agree with you put the phone down on her. You really are a shit.-▬▬▬▬▬▬▬▬▬▬▬▬▬▬

Somebody who has witnessed you behaviour recently described you as a baby throwing your toys out of the pram-samething Leslie described you as, after witnessing you, some 20 years ago.You should pay Kerina out of all the money you are getting from the rent for no.12. You should return no 12 and let my parents live there. They need to be on one level-dick head, and if that doesn't suit them they

Plate 14. Brotherly love email (continued on next page).

want to sell it and buy a garden flat and get out of your clutches. The despicable way you carried on over the carpet you ought to be ashamed of yourself-putting the phone down on Renata bullying her over your rotten carpet saying that you would only allow her to have it if she went through the hassle of having the flat decorated.All this unpleasenatness went on for months, but you always behave like that. You did it over Renata's 90 bitrthday and my father's 90. You are like Hitler- and Renata could not stand up to you and you knowing this kept her enslaved all these years-You will have to pay for your sins in the next life make no mistake of that. ▬▬▬▬▬▬▬▬▬▬▬▬▬▬▬▬▬ To have given my name to the baillifs or rather to Kernanhan knowing full well why they wanted it for beggars belief to be so revengeful and nasty to your own brother-You are sick and then to deny you did it saying you didn't but Kernhan did. I had already given 81 to that shit if he wanted to w=communicate with me. If that is true then you are saying that Kernahan who is purely your agent did something against your wishes and you should deduct the £500 from their fees and send me the money. You could never admit a fault and thus you will remaind a bay for the rest of your life.

Plate 14. Brotherly love email (concluded).

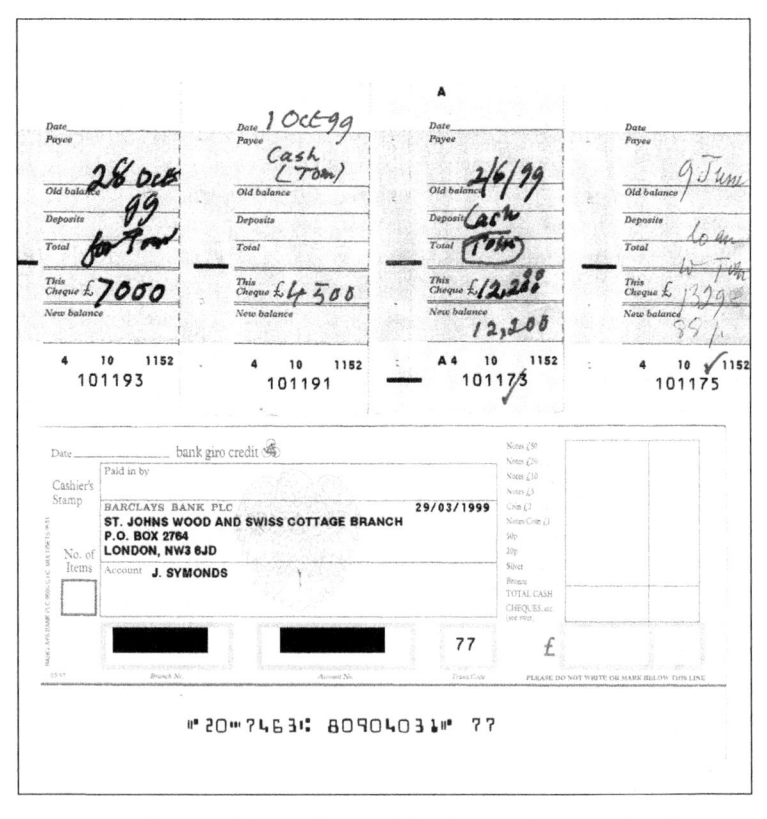

Plate 15. Some of John Symonds's cheque book stubs showing cash gifts and one loan to Tommy.

Plate 16. New temporary cross and memorial on John and Renata Symonds's otherwise neglected grave.

Plate 17. Tommy aged 66.

7

THE DEATH OF JOHN SYMONDS

THE BEGINNING OF the end of our parents was on an ill-fated day in July 2005. Mother was doing the ironing—the ironing board was in the entrance hall just outside the kitchen—when the phone rang. In her anxiety to answer it promptly she reached forwards through the open door of the kitchen to the phone which was on the sideboard. As she did so, her foot caught in the stand of the ironing board and, in her own words, she 'went flying'. The result was a broken hip. An ambulance took her to the nearby Royal Free Hospital. The treatment for this emergency is prompt operative fixation of the break followed by getting up and about as soon as practicable with the help of physiotherapy. Normally, such patients would be out of hospital in a few days.

But now, the great British National Health Service gets into action. Or rather, it doesn't. Mother suffered from angina (chest pain, typically brought on by exertion, cold weather, or anxiety, resulting from narrowing of the coronary arteries). She had been under the care of an excellent private cardiologist in Harley Street whom she saw regularly, and was being treated successfully with medicines taken by mouth.

However, in the hospital when they heard she had a heart condition, before proceeding with the operation they thought they needed the opinion of a hospital cardiologist. It took *ten days* for one to be found—who promptly pronounced her fit for a general anaesthetic. This delay was inexcusable. In the meantime mother was in bad pain and was being treated with pain-killers which didn't work effectively and caused side-effects. When she eventually came home—after three-and-a-half weeks instead of the usual three to five days—she said, 'I've been to hell and back.' She was never the same after that.

Since I was living in Japan there was little I could do except try to advise by phone and email. What about Tommy arranging for mother to be treated privately—for which if necessary I would pay—so they would get on with the operation? As a matter of principle he would take up no suggestion of mine. So mother languished in the public hospital.

That wasn't the only problem. Father was then aged 91. He was frail, quite deaf, and incapable of looking after himself. But by a fortunate coincidence my eldest son, George, was staying with them. He manfully fulfilled the role of carer for his grandfather, and thus the immediate crisis was resolved. But George couldn't stay indefinitely—he had already postponed his travel plans—so other arrangements had to be made to look after father. Unfortunately, as no cooperation from Tommy was forthcoming I sent him a fax on 21 July 2005.

> This is a family emergency. For God's sake we must put aside our differences to deal with the situation in the best way we can.
>
> The immediate problem is what to do about Daddy. We cannot expect George to look after him for more than a few days. As you know he cancelled his flight on Wednesday to help his Grandfather but wishes to leave soon. Therefore, we need to organise private day and night nurses to look after him at No 81. Or perhaps you could take him to your house and look after him there with the help of private nurses. It should hardly be necessary to add that if he is put into a nursing home or geriatric ward it will kill him!
>
> Since you are doubtless unwilling to share the cost of this, I will pay for private nursing and home help myself. The same goes for hospital treatment. If it would speed things up, or if Mummy would be more comfortable being treated privately (or perhaps moving to a private room in the Royal Free Hospital if they have such), I will pay for this too. Since you are the man on the ground you must organise this immediately and let me know what is going on.

I followed this up with a phone call. Incredibly, all I got from Tommy was abuse. The only thing I could think of doing then was to send another fax:

> Your rudeness to me and your selfishness are of an extreme degree. I am afraid this behaviour shows you must be actually mad or, to put it more charitably, you are pitiable.
>
> As I have already told you, this is a family emergency. Don't you understand this?
>
> I hope that when you are old—you are already quite old—and if you are in trouble, your son will not treat you as you treat our parents.
>
> I must repeat—unless you wish our father to die—the only sensible thing is for you to take him to stay with you in your house. I will take care of all your out-of-pocket expenses.
>
> I beg you to put aside your resentment, try to break out of your self-absorption, and give this matter your top priority.

This fax was promptly sent back to me with the following words scribbled at the bottom: 'Return my Dictionary and the £500 you stole from me.' See Plate 4. (The £500 parking fine which he had had to pay he accused me of 'stealing' from him!)

It later emerged that Tommy had an answer, of a sort, to deal with this crisis. He had a girlfriend, Carole, who would live at No 81 and look after father. Carole was a young black woman—with a 10 month old baby and a 9 year old child by a different man. She would be a carer for a modest payment. It would be hard to think of a less suitable arrangement for father. For one thing, he didn't particularly like black people.

However, by a minor miracle, working the phone from Tokyo, I was able to arrange for a professional carer, a Philippine lady called Carina, to come in for one week, this being the maximum time she could spare. After that, however, Carole with her baby and child would hold the fort until mother was released from the hospital.

Fax to Tommy, 27 July 2005:

This is a preliminary report about the arrangements I have made. You have got to understand that Daddy has to have 24-hour professional help. It is no good talking about people from the Council or from private agencies coming in for a short time in the morning and evening. What happens if it is in the evening or night and he is by himself and wants a hot water bottle or a glass of milk and starts wandering around and falls? Have you thought of that?

I have arranged for Carina, whom I understand you met this morning, to come full-time from Monday next and stay for one week in the first instance. This has Mummy's full agreement. And whether Carina comes or not I have promised to pay her. You don't seem to realise how difficult it is to find someone like her at short notice and how lucky it is that that I have found her.

George will be leaving next Tuesday morning come hell or high water. He has already gone far beyond the call of duty which is more than one can say for you. Since you have been completely uncooperative towards me over this family emergency, I have taken on the responsibility of making suitable arrangements independently, and I would thank you to go along with them and not interfere. If you wish to communicate with me about these and are prepared to discuss this matter only, feel free to do so.

Talking with Tommy on the phone at this point was singularly unrewarding: he was only interested in criticising and blaming me for all the wrongs he claimed I had done him. I therefore sent a detailed letter on 29 July 2005 about the problems between us:

Has it ever occurred to you that, maybe, once in your life, just once, you might be wrong? Our parents are in the middle of a major crisis. You are the man on the ground and the obvious person to take charge of the arrangements. But no. Your only concern, it seems, is money which you allege I owe you—with your voice shaking with nervousness you want to talk about that instead of the urgent matter of our parents' very bad situation and how to help it.

For you to claim against me the cost of a parking fine and subsequent penalties which you incurred for £500 is contemptible. You seem to think I should have colluded with you in a criminal act: giving a false address to Camden Council. You had enough time—I warned you repeatedly about this over several months—to sort the matter out and pay the fine. I did not give your address to Camden Council, nor would I have done, because I did not and do not wish to see you in prison. However, I did pass your address to Kernahans when they requested it in order to stop my tenants being repeatedly troubled by visits from bailiffs and frequent letters addressed to you at my flat. What honest objection could you have had to that? In any case, why didn't you mention this before? Why did you wait till there is a family emergency and I called you, before you raised it?

Your extraordinary and dishonest behaviour which resulted in visits from the bailiffs and letters from enforcement agencies addressed to you at my flat, so upset my tenants that they moved out and the flat was unoccupied for six weeks. If you persist in your outrageous claim that I stole from you £500 which you had to pay for a parking fine, I will make a counter claim that you stole from me six weeks' rent, which is £1,500 x 1½ = £2,250, so *you* owe *me* £2,250.

As for the *Dictionary*, let me to make one or two points clear. It has been in my possession for around fifteen years. Why did you raise the matter only a few weeks ago? And why were you so cowardly as to ask Mummy to ask me instead of approaching me directly? And when you did approach me, it was as if you were a stranger, Thomas J Symonds, who sends an e-mail with a demand that [my wife] should be a delivery service for you! You said nothing about the serious rift in our relationship which you caused over a year ago and which ended with you shouting at me in an abusive manner on the telephone when I was seeking your help with Daddy's 90th birthday celebration!

This behaviour is almost unforgivable, but let us put it aside for the moment and talk about the *Dictionary*.

I understand the *Dictionary* is jointly owned by Daddy and you.[16] When this matter came up a few weeks ago Daddy told me on the telephone very clearly that he did not want the Dictionary back and that I may keep it. But you have a half share. Well, I will buy you out. How much do you think the *Dictionary* is worth?

To return to more immediate matters, I wish to make it clear that when I said I will pay for all our parents' care, home help, nursing etc., I meant it only in the sense of assisting with cash flow. By rights, you must surely agree, such expenses should be shared equally between us. [I might have added that there was no reason why our parents couldn't pay for such expenses from their own funds.]

While we are on the subject of money, I have to say it is shocking that you put your hand out to our aged mother to the tune of £25,000 about three years ago. This was a big chunk out of her life savings: her security in her old age for circumstances such as these which she and Daddy are now facing. I doubt you have paid back much or any of this loan in these three years. It is a pity you didn't ask me for help if you were short of bread—I would not have turned you down. As for assisting with the parental crisis, don't worry. You have done a minimum, which is better than nothing, but from now on I will do all that is needed as far as I can from Japan without the pleasure of your cooperation. It is outrageous that you expected George to stay and look after Daddy until Mummy is back on her feet, if she ever will be. George is leaving on Tuesday 2 August and I suggest you go along

---

16 This was not the case, as shown on page 58.

with the arrangements I have set up for a live-in home help. Incidentally, Daddy doesn't want to live with you, and I don't blame him.

Having said all that, I should like to add that life is short, we are both getting old and our parents obviously cannot have much life ahead of them. You have to face the fact that this crisis may finish them off quite soon. It is, therefore, most regrettable that you persist in behaving towards me with such enmity. I have no ill feelings towards you, Tom. Rather, I feel very sorry that you cling to your anger from real or imagined slights going back *decades*. This is not good for your soul, or mine. For God's sake, while our parents and we are still alive—and there may be very little time left—I beg you to put aside your anger, let go of past grievances, and let us try, even at this late stage, to have a better brotherly relationship!

I might have saved myself the trouble of writing this. And with the benefit of hindsight, what I *should* have done is to have given Tommy one warning that he must immediately pay the fine and give the correct address of the place where he keeps his car, or I will without further notice inform Camden Council of the facts. Actually, I had a civic duty to do this, as failure to report a suspected crime might have meant that I could have been regarded as an accessory after the fact. But poor Shmoogie needed to be protected from nasty big brother—Camden Council!

***

When father reached his late 80s his health declined markedly. He was quite deaf, mildly confused, and suffered increasing physical weakness. Part of the reason for this was a series of mini-strokes caused through an irregular heart beat. He had difficulty in swallowing, as a result of which he developed aspiration pneumonia and was admitted to hospital. During one admission in September 2006, a month before he died, I managed to take time off from my clinic and travel to London.

I went with mother to see him. He was in the multi-bedded male geriatric ward at the Royal Free Hospital, which he hated. The ward was understaffed. I was there when father called out, 'Nurse, nurse, can I have a cup of tea, please.' The nurse replied, 'All right, all right, wait a minute and I'll bring you some tea.' Twenty minutes later: no tea. Father was by that time bedbound and could only manage pureed food. He was desperate to come home, but the hospital, not unreasonably, didn't want to release him, or it seemed as if they even had some kind of legal hold on him (!), until the home circumstances met their approval. Fortunately, I was able to contact Carina again, and she with a nurse friend agreed to come in once more as the carers. But first, these two ladies had to go to the trouble of presenting themselves to the hospital discharge committee (or whatever it was called) so they could be satisfied that appropriate twenty-four-hour professional help was available if father went home. This being the case, the hospital agreed to release him. While these negotiations were going on, Tommy was in constant attendance: it seemed his aim was to *prevent* father being released back home.

Pending his return by ambulance, mother and I were busy with the preparations in the bedroom on the second floor. A hospital bed had been installed and supplies of special food, incontinence pants, etc., were stocked up. The two nurses were had arrived: they would sleep in the attic room and be available day and night. That, anyway, was the plan.

In the middle of these activities Tommy turned up unannounced and let himself in with his key. He immediately started aggressively questioning one of the carers, who was in the kitchen: 'What are you doing here?' he demanded to know. 'I've come to look after your father,' she replied. Hearing this, I went downstairs intending to get him to leave, but I suffered a sudden physical assault from him. Mother then appeared, greatly distressed, wailing, 'This is a nightmare, this is a nightmare!' At this, Tommy came to his senses and ran out of the door. I followed, not to get my revenge—I would not strike my own brother—but to make sure he had left and was outside the front door of the house. This incident was so upsetting that I called the police. A male and female officer attended and took a statement. As a result, they visited Tommy and temporarily confiscated his keys to my flat, cautioning him not come again until I had left to return to Japan.

When the police were present we were all sitting in the living room. And mother, nodding her head, repeated several times—it sounded almost like a mantra—'I have a very good relationship with my younger son.'

At about 9.00 pm an ambulance turned up with father. He was carried upstairs and put to bed in his own room. He expressed *enormous relief and joy* to be back home: 'I want a glass of champagne!' he cried. I went out in search of some but could only find a bottle of sparkling wine at a nearby convenience store.

The next day I had to leave. I kissed my father goodbye, knowing I would never see him again.

During this time I had been in contact with the GP, Dr Lucia Grun. She knew all about the situation and agreed that *John should be allowed to die at home*. Alas, this was not to be.

A few days later Dr Grun visited him and found everything under control. But in the middle of the following night John apparently again had difficulty breathing. Our dear mother, instead of alerting the carers in the room above, or phoning *me*, called Tommy. She had been coached for this and her next move, as instructed by Tommy, was to call an ambulance. An ambulance soon arrived and took him back to the hospital! The carers apparently slept through it all. As a result they were dismissed—not that they needed much encouragement to leave because, as they told me afterwards, they had been subjected to harassment from Tommy in the meantime.

Thus, father was re-admitted to hospital. A day or two later the crisis had resolved and he was back to square one: stuck in hospital, hating every moment, and begging to go home. This was related to me by my daughter who visited him and by the helpful downstairs neighbour, Michael Haag, who also saw him in the hospital.

Knowing the impossibility of getting Tommy bestir himself and find new carers, I appealed in a fax to Burnett, the above-mentioned family accountant and supposed impartial friend, to intervene:

> I spoke to a doctor at the Royal Free Hospital about my father. The situation is that he has recovered from the immediate medical problem but cannot go home until suitable arrangements for home care are once more set up. As he is now bed-bound this means he will need two full-time carers who cannot be provided by the NHS or local council. Therefore we shall have to pay for these arrangements privately. As you know, my parents have ample funds in their joint Woolwich Guernsey account [It was £147,246 in April 2003: see Plate 5] and this is precisely what they have been saving their money for. The alternative is that father will die in hospital. He is begging to come home and surely should be helped to use his own money so that he can spend his last days as he wishes.
>
> The two carers who were there before I am sure will not want to come again—they were very upset and frightened by Tom's behaviour. So we have to contact a nursing agency to find new carers.
>
> To complicate matters further, mother has the early stages of dementia and suffers from severe short-term memory loss. As far as I can ascertain she has not been living at 81 Belsize Lane for the last several days and presumably is staying with Tom—I am glad he is doing at least some good by looking after our mother. But I have been unable to speak to her since the telephone is never answered.
>
> As you know, the relationship between Tom and me has completely broken down. The police had to be called when he assaulted me in my own home recently.

Unfortunately, it seems that Tom's involvement with our parents is to a large extent motivated by self-interest. Taking advantage of a confused elderly woman, he has induced her to part with tens of thousands of pounds[17] in the last few years, and all the signs are that he does not want our parents to spend their own money on themselves. Indeed, he seems to be taking active steps to prevent them doing so—in order to obtain a larger inheritance!

This is confirmed in Tommy's own words by a notice on his letterhead dated 28 April 2005 which he left at No 81 for our parents. It contains eleven numbered instructions to them on how not to be influenced by me! Point number 9 is: 'Gabriel only wants to get rid of your money so there is nothing for me.' (Plate 6.) My fax, in which I refer to this memorandum, continued:

> Why should there be any money left for Tom, or me for that matter? Why should our parents be obstructed in spending *their own money on themselves* at this time of their greatest need? Please do what you can about this, and let me know what is happening.

I had earlier mentioned to Burnett my concern that the pending breakdown of the relationship between Tommy and me could result, when the time came, in him making off with our parents' goods and chattels as well as grabbing all their money. Burnett assured me—falsely as it turned out—that he 'will not allow this to happen.'

Although all four of us were his paying clients, he was not merely an agent, doing what was told: he was the long-

---

[17] For example, when I visited London in September 2006, with mother's permission I examined those records that were available (it is not a complete list) of her NatWest bank current account and found the following withdrawals had been made in favour of Tommy. For 2001: £10,000; 2002: £34,000; 2004: £6,000; 2005: £6,000; and 2006: £10,500.

standing trusted family accountant, financial and quasi-legal advisor, and to a certain extent, a friend—or so I believed.

I had had a gut feeling of potential problems with this man from a note in my diary about a phone conversation with father on 26 February 1998:

> I expressed reservations about Clive Burnett being an executor and trustee of his and mother's wills, since there is a potential conflict of interest as he is Tommy's accountant too; he didn't agree.

How did the family get involved with this man? He came through Tommy—always a dubious recommendation. Previously, our parents had had wills drafted by a local solicitor, but then they were persuaded to hand everything over to Burnett. Mother had what I thought was exaggerated respect for and deference to him. He was a chartered accountant but, lacking an office, worked from home and through his mobile phone, and sometimes by visiting clients. He would call on our parents to discuss their end-of-year accounts; this he did having plunked his phone beside him while he munched through smoked salmon and cream cheese snacks my mother had lovingly prepared for him. It has to be said he performed his work as an accountant efficiently, and was certainly helpful in my acquisition of No 12 as related above. However, as subsequent events showed, he was in Tommy's pocket.

Memorial service for John Symonds
As already mentioned, having been given only three day's notice to attend father's funeral, of course it was impossible to make it in time all the way from Japan. I therefore decided to hold a separate memorial service for him at Highgate Cemetery where he was buried.

After John's death mother was living with Tommy and I was prevented from having any contact with her; she was essentially a prisoner in his house. There were a few patients who out of loyalty still consulted her so from time to time she was brought to No 81 to see them.

On 8 February 2007 I travelled to London for the memorial service which I had arranged. On the evening of the day when I arrived at No 81 an unfortunate incident occurred—there have been so many of these!

I let myself in and after a while a client of my mother's rang the bell. I told her there must have been a mistake about the appointment as my mother was not there, and she went away. Then I went to talk to the neighbours in the basement, Michael Haag and his wife.

Suddenly there was a noise of footsteps from the hall above. Wondering what was going on, I went to investigate. I came upon mother being led along the hallway by Tommy, and I confronted them. But mother appeared not recognise me. I asked her to come in and talk to me. She mumbled, 'I can't, I can't.' Then without a word Tommy turned her around to lead her back out of the front door. I didn't want to create a scene and upset her, much less for her to be involved in tug-of-war.

That was the last time I saw my poor mother standing on her own feet. Tommy had total control over her and guarded her from any contact with me. How easily he could have taken a different attitude and cooperated with me! 'Yes Mummy, here's Gabriel. You go in with him and call me when you want me to fetch you.' He showed no magnanimity, no openness of heart, no generosity—no *love*.

My son Matthew turned up later that night from Portsmouth where he was studying at the university. The next day we got up early for the Memorial Service. I had arranged for a car to take the people who were going to attend to Highgate Cemetery. We arrived at 7.15 am. It was already light, there was snow on the ground and it was quite cold. A man working in the grounds let us in by arrangement and we drove down to the end of the track in the Eastern Cemetery near to where John Symonds lies buried. I assembled my bagpipes (I had acquired some facility on this instrument during the last few years in

Tokyo) and played *Amazing Grace* as we walked the rest of the way to the grave. We stopped there and the six mourners gathered around. I gave my welcoming speech, and then each person read a short passage from one of John Symonds's works, and Matthew read the Prayer of St Francis in Italian. My contribution at this point was to play on the highland bagpipes a traditional lament, *The Flowers of the Forest*, after which we held a two minutes' silence. Then I read from Revelations 21:1-8. We ended with The Lord's Prayer, and I played a slow march, *Scots Wha Ha'e*, as we walked back to the car. It was a moving occasion and I felt I had done what I needed to do to pay my last respects to my father. Later we all had breakfast at a café in Belsize Lane.

This was the order of the proceedings:

MEMORIAL CEREMONY FOR
JOHN SYMONDS
(1914 – 2006)
Highgate Cemetery
Friday 9th February 2007 at dawn

1. Welcome and introductory remarks – Gabriel Symonds
2. Four readings from John Symonds's works, and prayer
   The Bright Blue Sky (1956) – Michael Haag
   The Isle of Cats (1955) – Vicki Harding
   Poem (Untitled, c 1934) – Loutfia Haag
   Poem (Untitled, c 1934) – Robert Deane
   Prayer of St Francis – Matthew Symonds, read in Italian
3. Lament, 'The Flowers of the Forest – Gabriel Symonds, played on the Highland Bagpipes
4. Two minutes' silence
5. Reading from Revelations 21:1-8
6. The Lord's Prayer
7. Each person will lay a white rose upon the grave, and depart.

My opening remarks were these:

Dear Friends and Matthew,

Thank you very much for coming here so early on this cold morning.

This gathering is not intended as a second funeral, but as a brief memorial service for John Symonds. All of you except Matthew and I were present at his funeral last November. Unfortunately, it was not possible for me to be present at that time, and I wish to pay my last respects to my father by this ceremony today. It is also good that Matthew can say his goodbyes to his grandfather today too.

In one of John's early novels, *The Bright Blue Sky*, from which there will be a short reading in a little while, he quotes Seneca: 'Death is sadness, not for the dead but for the living.' And indeed it is. However, there is not just one sadness: there are three, or rather I should say, there are three *wrongs*, in relation to John's death of which I wish to speak.

In the last few weeks of his life, when he was enfeebled by old age and illness to the point of total physical helplessness, his dying was marred by one fact which was obvious to all who visited him at his hospital bed: that he *was* in hospital instead of his own home, where he desperately wished to be. Unfortunately, this wish was ignored, or worse, deliberately over-ridden for reasons which bring no credit on the one who had it in his power to accede to his wish, and he died in the hospital.

That was the wrong of omission done to John.

John was a great diarist. For more that half a century he kept a diary—the unique written story of his life and most personal expression of his thoughts and feelings to the events in which he was involved and which he observed. A few days before he died, these dairies, apart from a few for which I was able to arrange safe-keeping, were unlawfully removed from his home.

That was the first wrong of commission done to John.

In the year 2000, when he was in relatively good health and still mentally competent, he drafted a will in which, in a perfectly reasonable and normal way, he stated his desire that, among other provisions, the rights in all his published and unpublished works including his diaries should be bequeathed in equal shares to his two sons. Although I do not know for certain if this will was completed (I assumed it had been), its whereabouts, if it still exists, are at present unknown to me. However, in mid-2005, which was a mere 17 months before my father died, when he was suffering from dementia and marked deafness, he was pressured or tricked into signing a new will which entirely excluded me as an executor and as a beneficiary from his estate.

That was the second wrong of commission done to John.

The first wrong cannot be undone; the second and third wrongs may, perhaps, with the help of the legal profession in this country, be put to rights to accord with John's wishes as expressed in his will of 2000.

Having now spoken about these matters in public and given them due weight, before all of you as witnesses, I hope that my dear father, grandfather of Matthew, beloved husband to my mother Renata, and former friend to all who are gathered here, may rest in peace.

I then read the moving and uplifting words of Revelations 21:1–8

> I saw a new heaven and a new earth: for the first heaven and the first earth have passed away, and the sea is no more. I saw the holy city, New Jerusalem, coming down out of heaven from God, made ready like a bride adorned for her husband. I heard a loud voice out of heaven saying, 'Behold, God's dwelling is with people, and he will dwell with them, and they will be his people, and God himself will be with them as their God. He will wipe away from them every tear from their eyes. Death will be no more; neither will there be mourning, nor crying, nor pain, any more. The first things have passed away.' He who sits on the throne said, 'Behold, I am making all things new.' He said, 'Write, for these words

of God are faithful and true.' He said to me, 'It is done! I am the Alpha and the Omega, the Beginning and the End. I will give freely to him who is thirsty from the spring of the water of life. He who overcomes, I will give him these things. I will be his God, and he will be my son. But for the cowardly, unbelieving, sinners, abominable, murderers, sexually immoral, sorcerers, idolaters, and *all liars*, their part is in the lake that burns with fire and sulfur, which is the second death.'

There was no mistaking at whom the words I have italicised in the last verse were aimed.

8
THE DEATH OF RENATA SYMONDS

AFTER THE SHAMEFUL episode in February 2007 when mother was taken away by Tommy to prevent her meeting me, I knew she would not survive long. At that time she was frail, confused, with severe memory impairment, and completely under Tommy's control. She lived in his house so he decided who was allowed to visit her and who was not.

As an example of mother's memory loss, she would occasionally ring me up and then immediately ask me to tell her my phone number! Talking with her she would often forget in the middle of a sentence what she had said at the beginning. Nonetheless, her memory for events in the distant past was well preserved.

On 4 March 2007, a mere three months before she died, our dear mother executed a new will to disinherit me and my family and leave everything to Tommy (except for a bequest of £2,000 to Maureen). In preparation for this change of heart, on 21 January 2007 she was taken on a two hours' car drive out of London, accompanied by Tommy and Burnett, to Crowthorne in Berkshire to meet a lawyer called Stirling Halliday (he refers to himself in the document below as SHG) who was in cahoots with Burnett. This was for the purpose of determining that mother was competent to make a new will in case I should later challenge it.

I did indeed investigate whether I had grounds in law to challenge this will, but discovered, as is so often the case with lawsuits, it was likely to be a difficult, time-consuming, and expensive business. It was not as if millions were at stake: the amount of money involved was something in excess of £110,000 and our parents' goods and chattels were largely of sentimental value. There were, however, the copyrights of their published and unpublished works. Over the years since John Symonds's death I had received a number of enquiries from publishers interested republishing some of his works, but without the copyrights issue being determined by grant of probate on his will, this would not have been possible; in any case there would probably be little money in such a venture.

The document prepared by Stirling Halliday was in the form of an Attendance Note reproduced below in italics. My comments on it for my solicitor, written 15 April 2015, were as follows:

> Apart from being badly written and containing various colloquialisms which seem out of place in a legal document, this is not a *Larke v. Nugus* statement. [A statement relating to all the circumstances, as far as the solicitor is aware of them, surrounding the will.] The Note gives opinion but very little evidence on which it is based.
>
> *SGH in attendance with Tom Symonds, Renata Symonds and Clive Burnett.*
>
> Why were Tom Symonds and Clive Burnett in attendance? If Renata was competent and wished to change her will, she surely could have done this without the presence of two other people who had a vested interest in her drafting a new will. The Note also contains a number of inaccuracies and presents a misleadingly one-sided picture:
>
> *The meeting had been called as a consequence of fears that the Will completed by Renata in 2005 might well be challenged on Renata's death by…Gabriel.*
>
> Whose fears? Clearly Tom's, not Renata's. Was Renata so fearful that she wished to go to the trouble of travelling to Crowthorne to see a solicitor to build a defence of evidence to use against me in case I should challenge her latest will? The idea is preposterous.

SGH, who has spoken with Renata, Tom and Gabriel in the past, is au fait with the 'family structure' having handled...John and Renata's sale of 81 Bellsize Lane...

81 Bellsize Lane is wrong apart from being misspelt; he means 12 Belsize Court. He may have spoken to Renata in the past but it wasn't about her will, and I believe this was the first time they met.

Stirling Halliday had advised me a few years previously on the matter of father being sued by the Ordo Templi Orientis. I instructed Stirling Halliday to review the case— for which I paid him £3,000. I never spoke to him of family relationships so what does he mean by 'family structure' and how did he learn of it? I sent him a letter dated 25 January 2007 warning him that if he acted for Burnett and/or Thomas against me I would consider it a conflict of interest; there was no acknowledgement or reply.

In any case, up till 2003 there was a reasonably normal fraternal relationship between Thomas and me, and a normal accountant-client relationship between Burnett and me till around the time of father's death in 2006.

Although SGH has understood that relations between Tom and Gabriel were sometimes strained, it was clear as a consequence of our meeting that those relations had in fact deteriorated substantially.

He knew this anyway from my letter, so why, under these circumstances, did he act for Thomas with Burnett's collusion?

Tom has essentially adopted responsibility for looking after Renata.

This is debateable. Renata was almost certainly pressured by Tom to live with him. She would surely have wished to continue in the home (actually my home) where she had lived with John for the last twenty years in familiar surroundings with all her possessions and where she still saw her clients. It is well known that elderly people put into a new environment rapidly become confused and their health deteriorates, and this is what happened.

Renata confirms that she had been very disappointed so far as Gabriel's actions were concerned after the death of John, particularly as to a disagreement that would appear to have arisen as to John's diaries.

This is so far-fetched it is unbelievable. If Renata allegedly had been 'very disappointed…particularly as to a disagreement [over] John's diaries' then *what else* was she disappointed over? In any case, she could have told me directly if she was in any way disappointed with me; she never did. Yet we are expected to believe this is her reason for disinheriting me!

What is beyond dispute, however, is the fact that in the last eight months or so of her life Renata was totally controlled by Thomas. On one occasion when I did manage to speak with her on the phone, I could hear Thomas in the background urging her: '*Tell him to return the diaries! Tell him to return the diaries!*' It is perfectly clear that Thomas repeatedly coached our mother to say to Stirling Halliday whatever he (Thomas) wanted her to say. On other occasions when I called and asked to speak to my mother, Thomas answered the phone and immediately hung up. There was never any suggestion that my mother felt strongly about my possession of a few of the diaries and it is preposterous to assert that she wanted to disinherit me and my family for this reason.

SGH queried Clive as to how he had prepared John and Renata's Wills back in 2005. Clive confirms that all he had done upon John and Renata's instruction was to arrange for the Wills to be 're-typed' used a precedent document from the previous year that had been prepared by Solicitors.

What solicitors? It was all done by Burnett using a pro-forma document he found somewhere.

SGH was aware that there was some contention on Gabriel's behalf as to the legitimacy of the Last Will and Testament of John...Clive confirmed (and Renata supports Clive in these comments) that this is the primary reason for our meeting today, because Renata does not want a situation to arise in the future where her intentions as to the disposal of her estate should be challenged.

Note 'Clive confirmed'. This is evidence that Thomas and Burnett were orchestrating the meeting. And the testator was a 93 year old lady with documented confusion and memory impairment, but who was nonetheless so farsighted that she wanted to avoid her firstborn son challenging being disinherited! Clearly, this is Thomas's doing.

Bottom line, Renata is essentially content with the document...

This is careless writing. What does it mean, 'essentially content'? In the main content? Then why was she not fully content?

[Renata] does not think...it would be wise for Gabriel to be involved in how her body is dealt with (sic) after her death and more particularly the Church service.

Why did Renata think, or not think, this? Whence comes the suggestion I might be unhappy over the disposal of her body as stated in her will? Clearly from Thomas who wanted to exclude me from anything to do with our mother—even after her death!

Other than a specific gift which is to be made to a friend 'Maureen' she wants all of her assets on death to pass to Tom and if Tom predeceases her then it (sic) is to pass to Tom's child, Toby.

Maureen is Toby's mother; but it is incredible that Renata, who had a close and loving relationship with my wife, our three children, and me, would *in her right mind* have wanted to leave them and me nothing.

Renata makes it clear to SGH that is not her intention to spite Gabriel...

I am sure it was not her intention, but with this will it rather looks like it.

...she has concluded that Gabriel is comfortable (financially), that Tom has committed a vast amount of time and attention to her and her late husband and that...she should make sure that he [Thomas] is properly catered for (sic).

So now we have an additional alleged reason for cutting my family and me out of her will. But how did Renata conclude I was comfortably off? She knew nothing of my financial affairs. 'Tom has committed a vast amount of time and attention to her and her late husband', so he deserved to inherit her entire estate? The implication is that I did nothing for them. Quite the contrary: John and Renata visited Japan yearly since 1984 to stay with me and my family, always travelling business class paid for by me. In addition, I spent a lot of money on them for new furniture and household equipment, private medical fees and chemist's bills, many birthday presents, a substantial amount towards the cost of a new car, payment for carers to look after John when Renata was in hospital, jewellery for my mother, bespoke clothes for my father, etc., etc., and *they lived rent-free for twenty years in my flat.* Also, I and or my wife and three children visited London two or three times a year over many years to see them. Furthermore, I never asked them for a penny, whereas Thomas obtained numerous sums of money from them over the years.

As far as I could judge, Thomas was a successful publisher and antiquarian bookseller and it is nonsense for SGH to imply that Thomas was in a state of penury and needed to be 'catered for'.

> *SGH is clear in his own mind that Renata fully appreciates and understands her instruction, her intentions are very clearly elucidated to SGH, her feelings and views on the issue are unchallengeable…SGH had no doubt that she fully appreciated what she was doing…It was also clear that Renata knew her own mind*

These are merely assertions which remain as such no matter how many times they are repeated in different words. What is the evidence on which they are based?

> *SGH asked Clive and Tom to leave the room, so that SGH could have a private word with Renata…*

It is hardly credibly that Renata would confide privately to SHG if she wasn't happy about the proposed new will, having been brought to his office by Thomas and Burnett for the specific purposed of disinheriting me, bearing in mind that she lived with Thomas and was totally under his control.

Sans everything
How did it come about that our parents' savings at that time of over £110,000 in the Woolwich Building Society in Guernsey were taken out from there (except for a balance of £500) and transferred to mother's current account at the NatWest bank, whence of that money £100,000 was promptly paid into Burnett's client account? Clearly, mother of her own volition had no reason to make these transfers. It is obvious that she was put up to it by Tommy with the collusion and assistance of Burnett. Why not leave our parents' savings where they were, and after they died the cash could be disbursed according to their wills? The reason is that Tommy wanted to grab it all for himself. It was easier for him to do this if he could argue it was a lifetime gift. But was it really a gift? It appears that mother, in her confused and forgetful state, signed anything that was put in front of her—then promptly forgot she had done so.

If further evidence is needed of our mother being subjected to undue influence by Tommy it is provided in a notepad (of which I have photographic copies) which she used to remind herself of recent events and as a 'to do' list. During my visit to London in 2006 I was able to draw her attention to certain facts of which she appeared to be unaware. These were, in particular, that she had in March 2006 signed a cheque in Tommy's favour for £10,000 (Plate 7); then she had signed bank documents to a joint account with Tommy (Plate 8); he was the main signatory, and any withdrawals she wished to make needed his counter-signature. When I explained this to her she was aghast and could not believe it. Forthwith we set out for the nearby NatWest bank. Yes, it was true; but this change could not be undone without Tommy's agreement!

Sadly, as I have recounted above, that visit to London was the last one I made while my father was alive. However, when I was back in Japan I was shocked to be informed that he had made a new will to disinherit me. This set me wondering whether mother, likewise, had redrafted her will for the same purpose. Talking with her on the phone during the short time it was possible to do this until access to her was blocked by Tommy, she refused to agree for me to see her last will. But she made the following written notes (Plate 9 shows one page):

> Clive has my money.
> Ask Clive, did father cut G[abriel] out of his will?!
> G wants copy of my will + wants me to have one as well
> Cl[ive] + Th[omas] are controlling my money—Buta haven't been paid—G has been informed (Buta is the tenants' association to which the service charge is payable.)
>
> Transfer my money back to Woolwich
> How much interest is Clive paying me?
> I want to see will in which G has been cut out of F[ather]'s will?!
> £40,000 I have given gifts to T[ommy].

> March this year [2006] £10,000 paid to T
> G wants to contest F's will—it was witnessed in wrong way
> Clive + Tom in cahoots
> G cut out from F's will
> G?? cut out from my [will]??
> All rights in his bks (books) to Th
> G no longer executor of F's will
> <u>My</u> will? Equal shares!

After father died I tried to question Burnett about why mother's savings were in his control and how much interest they were earing. (Banks and Building Societies like the offshore Woolwich Guernsey paid good interest in those days.) This what he said in an email of 14 January 2007:

> As far as the monies I am holding for Renata goes, these sums belong to her and have nothing to do with you and I will therefore not be answerable to you on it.

Now let's go back to Stirling Halliday's Attendance Note above. There we find that the reason for mother of her own free will and at her request to be dragged all the way to Crowthorne was to build a defence in case I should later challenge her will of 2005. If she made such a will in 2005 it would have been a mirror will of John's in which I am named as an executor but not as a beneficiary. And if this were the case then mother would have been aware of it, and to avoid the very situation she was allegedly anxious to avoid, would have had ample opportunity to say to me something along these lines:

> Gabriel, I'm sorry to tell you that I've decided to cut you *and your family* out of my will and leave everything to Shmoogie. The reason is that I'm *very disappointed* in your behaviour over retaining a few of father's diaries, so this is my way of showing my disapproval—although of course it's not to spite you. But even if you were to return the diaries now

it wouldn't make any difference because I believe you are a rich man. On the other hand, Shmoogie, in spite of being a successful antiquarian book dealer and publisher, living in a big house which he owns, and with a BMW car, and taking regular business trips to Europe and the US, and with him sending his son to a public school, and in spite of the tens of thousand of pounds we've given him over the last few years, is a poor man who needs to be *catered for*. Further, you've done nothing for us, apart from a few trifles such as allowing us to live rent-free for the last twenty years in your lovely flat, whereas Shmoogie has *essentially adopted responsibility* for looking after us. So please don't cause trouble by challenging my will after I die because these are my true wishes. And another thing…

Apart from the utter inconceivability of such behaviour on the part of our mother *in her right mind* (see the first Witness Statement in Chapter 10), Sterling Halliday's view of her mental capacity is dubious if we look at her medical records—I have copies of these.

First, there is the Discharge Summary from the Royal Free Hospital where mother was re-admitted from 11 February to 15 March 2007, a period of just under five weeks—indeed her last will was signed from her hospital bed on 4 March 2007. The list of diagnoses includes:

- Fracture of right pubic ramus (part of the hip bone) from another fall, and *dementia*.

Then we have her GP's records which contain the following statements:

- 9 Feb 2004: Memory deficit, probably dementia
- 18 July 2006: Memory is very poor
- 23 Jan 2007: Dementia seems worse
- 1 February 2007: She is obviously confused

- 10 March 2007: She has had a marked memory deficit since 2004 although she has never been formally assessed...I (Dr Lucia Grun) last saw her in January [2007] when her memory did seem to be significantly worse
- 23 March 2007: Mini-Mental State Examination (MMSE): Scored 22 out of 30 which suggests cognitive impairment.

Thus, mother's cognitive impairment including memory deficit, that is, dementia, was first documented in early 2004.

Last visit to my mother
All I could do from the other side of the world was to keep in touch with the social worker who was involved in mother's care and the staff of the Royal Free Hospital female geriatric ward. By mid-May 2007 it was clear that mother was dying. Indeed, she had little reason to live after the loss of her beloved husband the previous September. I therefore got myself to London as soon as I could to visit her in the hospital. But what if I were to meet Tommy there and, as would be very likely, he started making a scene? To deal with this possibility I went to the length of engaging the services of a professional bodyguard, Mr Phil Smith. I believe he was ex-special forces. His appearance was not particularly intimidating, but he had a look in his eye such that if he politely asked you to do something you didn't argue. It was just as well I made this arrangement for although I arrived in the morning as soon as the ward opened for visitors, Tommy was already there. However, Mr Smith induced Tommy to step outside the ward for ten minutes. Alas, mother by that stage was barely conscious but in obvious discomfort and moaning. I don't think she recognised me. Nonetheless, I said my last goodbyes. She passed away in the hospital two weeks later. At this final visit I was accompanied by Vicki Harding, a long-standing family friend.

But why was mother dying in a public geriatric ward instead of being in her own home at 81 Belsize Lane, cared for by private 24-hour nurses for which she had more than ample funds? *The shocking truth is that Tommy didn't allow it because, as in the case of our father, it would have reduced his inheritance!*

Memorial Service for Renata Symonds
Being unable to attend mother's funeral as explained in Chapter 6, later on I arranged a memorial ceremony for her; it followed the same format as for my father. This was the programme:

MEMORIAL CEREMONY FOR
RENATA SYMONDS
Born 7th August 1913, Cologne, Germany
Died 2nd June 2007, Hampstead, London, aged 93

Highgate Cemetery
Friday 5th December 2008 at 8.30 am

1. Welcome and introductory remarks – Gabriel Symonds
2. Readings from Renata Symonds's works, prayers, and remembrances
   Midlife: Problems and Solutions (1988) – Vicki Harding
   The Magic Mirror (1981), and remembrance – Sara Robin
   John Donne, No Man is an Island – Michael Haag
   Buddhist prayer – Masumi Symonds (in Japanese)
   Verse from the Koran – Loutfia Haag (in Arabic)
   Rainer Maria Rilke, The Unicorn – Alan Howlett
   Remembrance of Klaus Naumann – read by Gabriel Symonds
3. Lament, 'The Flowers of the Forest' – Gabriel Symonds (Highland Bagpipes)
4. Two minutes' silence
5. Reading: Revelations 21:1-8
6. All are invited to join in reciting The Lord's Prayer
7. Each person will lay a white rose upon the grave, and depart.

My opening remarks were as follows:

Dear Friends, Masumi, George, Matthew, and Erica,
Thank you for coming this cold December morning to be with me to pay our respects to Renata Symonds, my mother.

A number of you came here almost two years ago when we held a memorial service for my father, John Symonds. At that time you were aware of the rift in our family and the reason why I had been unable to attend his funeral. Unfortunately, this problem continued and indeed increased after John's death, so that it was also impossible for me to attend my mother's funeral.

It is strange, is it not, that a firstborn son should be unable to attend his mother's funeral?

At my father's memorial service, I spoke of three wrongs that had been done to him around the time of his death.

It is only proper that I should, for the record, and once again before all of you here as witnesses, similarly mention the wrongs that were done to Renata. As we cannot stay here all day, I shall mention only two.

Although I was in London on two occasions after John's death—before Renata was in a terminal state—I was prevented from meeting her by the scheming of one who put his own selfish ends and hatred of me above all else.

The second wrong that was done to my mother was that her own wishes were trampled upon. In particular, she made a will in 2000, when she was still in good health and in her right mind, in which she expressed the wish that her estate should be left in equal shares to her two sons. However, about three months before she died, when she was in a state of advanced senility, she was tricked or forced to sign a new will in which my name does not appear at all. I took legal advice over this matter and the upshot was that it would be very difficult and prohibitively expensive to try to reverse that state of affairs in a court of law, especially as her assets had almost certainly been removed from her control before her death.

It seems to me that truly there is a spirit of evil and madness that walks the earth.

I shall let that be.

Now, on a happier note, I would like to turn to some of mother's professional achievements. As you know, she was a Jungian psychotherapist who had a very successful private practice which she ran from her flat at 81 Belsize Lane for over twenty years.

Most of her working life was taken up with psychotherapy sessions with her many clients. She also gave many lectures, but left little in written form.

Some of her wisdom appears in her unpublished book *Midlife: Problems and Solutions*, from which an excerpt will be read shortly. Her only published work, as far as I am aware, is a monograph, *The Magic Mirror*, which contains the text of a lecture she gave in 1981 when she was a psychotherapist and senior counsellor at the Westminster Pastoral Foundation. An excerpt from this will also be read soon, and I should like to present each one of you with a copy afterwards.

The picture at the top of the programme is from a portrait of Renata which I commissioned from the well known portraitist Michael Taylor. It was completed in 2004 and exhibited at the Royal Society of Portrait Painters' Annual Exhibition in May 2005. I should like to quote from a press review: 'This ability to capture the character of the sitter as well as the moment in time is what makes a good portrait. Michael Taylor's painting of Renata Symonds, a nonagenarian Jungian psychotherapist, projected a lifetime of gravitas in her wise, intense gaze. But he has caught something else, a certain intellectual impatience, characterised by the swing of her hair, the angle of her head and her askew pearl necklace.' I think this sums up my mother quite well. Also, you will see in the background various objects that were important to Renata: the books on the shelf to her left—the Collected

Works of Jung—and a photo of Jung and one of her own analyst, Carol Jeffrey; and perhaps especially the lovely Ash tree visible through the window. Renata was very fond of this tree.

It is therefore fitting that this spot, with its many trees and birds, should be Renata's last resting place, beside her beloved husband, John.

May she rest in peace.

After the ceremony we all went to Kenwood House for breakfast. This was particularly appropriate because John and Renata often came to this splendid historical house for lunch.

9

STOLEN PORTRAIT AND FALSE WILLS

IN THE PREVIOUS chapter I mention the portrait of our mother that I commissioned from Michael Taylor in 2004 (the receipt is shown in Plate 10). After several visits to No 81 for sittings he produced a splendid work. It was shown, with my mother's and my permission, at the exhibition of the Royal Society of Portrait Painters in May 2005, and it appeared on the cover of the brochure (Plate 11). My intention then was to take the portrait back with me to Japan, but Michael Taylor wished also to show it at an exhibition called 'Home and Garden' to be held at the Jeffrye Museum in east London in 2007. The exhibition was of 'Paintings and Drawings of English, middle-class, urban domestic spaces, 1914 to 2006', and once again mother and I agreed.

Here is the scholarly description of the portrait from the catalogue:

> The painting depicts the enormous head (about twice life-size) of a 'head shrinker'. Though there might be a trend for facial close-ups that is amplified through the twentieth century, this large and meticulously portrayed face seems to have additional meanings. The close view might suggest that the therapist is larger than life for her patients, for whom she serves as a site for the projection of their fears and desires and with whom they play out their problematic relationships. Also, her hands are enlarged: Taylor claims to have made them reflect each other, as Symonds had written a psychoanalytic text about mirrors—mirrors show reflections, and similarly the therapist might reflect the emotional experience of her patients. While it might be read that the

sitter is squashed within her room and her space, she actually seems quite calm, pleased with her position. If anything, this depiction of Symonds shows her as unflinching. Her hands and eyes are experienced, adhering to the notion of the 'all-knowing therapist', but she is represented without expression. Perhaps Taylor portrays a person who has been hardened by her difficult life-experience; or perhaps Symonds maintains a neutral stance in her work as a therapist who must be a stable base around which others can share their varied thoughts.

While the depiction of Symonds' face comprises meticulous detail, the traces of her personal life and history are evidently not there but, rather, in the room. For instance, Symonds' tastes and autobiography can be traced in the shown books and in the photograph of a pupil of Jung (Carol Jeffrey) who helped Symonds to settle when she moved to London as a teenage refugee from Nazi Germany. The room, filled with her possessions, is endowed with her character. This is also emphasised by her unique dress—she is not wearing a suit or work outfit, but a particularly 'loud' pattern. In this room, Symonds uses her head, connecting with the thoughts and fantasies of others—perhaps only certain patients might feel comfortable in such a personal space, which to others could seem overpowering and might even influence their reflections and analyses. However, the blankness of Symonds' expression might counterbalance the personality of the room, enabling the patient to open up; similarly the painting also 'opens up' and generally reflects upon the relationship between domesticity and psychology. The work seems to suggest as strong connection between interior space and 'head space', between the domestic as a site of habitation but also of imagination and subjectivity. Jung in particular based his theories of the mind on dreams and stressed the importance of a shared unconscious life.

Thus the portrait was to be kept at my flat at No 81 till the date when it would again be exhibited to the public. However, on a brief visit to London that I made to see my parents in early 2006 I noticed the portrait was not to be found. I searched high and low but there was no sign of it. Where was it? I asked my mother, but being at this time of her life quite forgetful she had no idea about the portrait or its whereabouts. Then the penny dropped: Tommy had taken it away, that is, had stolen it. Unfortunately, by that time we weren't on speaking terms, so I asked him by email and letter if he had it. Yes, but mother had 'given' it to him! This was obvious nonsense. The portrait, commissioned and paid for by me, was my property. I certainly had not given it to my mother for her to dispose of. Therefore he must return the portrait immediately. He refused. Well, would he please at least release it for the exhibition, the catalogue for which had already been printed? Tommy's reply to this appeal (Plate 12) shows the reason, or one of the reasons, he took the portrait away. He wanted to use it as a kind of hostage to get me to do what he wanted: return the Johnson *Dictionary*, which didn't belong to him anyway, and to pressure me to give him the few volumes of our father's diaries that I had in my possession (see below).

The portrait wasn't the only property of mine he had unlawfully taken away from my flat: two cardboard boxes which I had prepared for shipping to Japan had been opened and a number of my books and various personal papers removed. At first he denied all knowledge of these items, but later they mysteriously turned at his home. The reason for this behaviour would soon become apparent.

John and Renata Symonds's estates

I had been given copies of our parents' wills that Burnett drafted in 2000. They were then in fairly good health and mentally competent. In the normal and reasonable way they stated their wishes that *their estates should be left in equal shares to Tommy and me*. The main assets were a not inconsiderable cash sum in a savings account, and potentially valuable copyrights of our parents' published and unpublished works.

During father's last admission to hospital and shortly before he died, I received word from my daughter, who was staying at No 81, that father's diaries—there were some fifty volumes—together with other property were in the process of being removed by Tommy. He had no right to do this especially as mother was still living. But Vicki, who also had a key to my flat, managed to retrieve for safe-keeping six volumes of the diaries which were piled up by the front door of the flat.

When Tommy found that some of the diaries were missing, it produced what can only be described as a *frenzy*. He was desperate to get his hands on *all* the diaries. A flurry of phone calls was made and emails sent to anyone who might know where they were. Burnett also involved himself and demanded that I reveal the whereabouts of those diaries, implying that they had been stolen and saying that he would inform the police if they were not produced! He also left an impertinent message containing veiled threats on Vicki's answering machine, and Tommy wanted to interrogate my daughter. My view was that until probate was granted Tommy had no more right to father's estate than I or anyone else. In any case, under the rules of inheritance father's estate passed to mother except for specific gifts.

The wills that were drafted by Burnett in 2000, of which I had been sent copies, I presumed had been properly executed, otherwise there would have been no point in making them. It then emerged that unbeknown to me father had made two later wills, again drafted by Burnett. There was a will of 2004 in which I was named as an executor but not a beneficiary, and in the last one, dated 28 May 2005, my name does not appear except as a meaningless afterthought:

> I desire that my funeral be conducted in accordance with the rites of the Church of England and in accordance with specific instructions given by my son Thomas who is to consult with his brother Gabriel with regard to the final arrangements.

Note that I am referred to merely as being Thomas's brother, not our father's elder son. John Symonds would never write like that and I suspect the reference to me was added as a sop by Burnett. Of course, Tommy never consulted with me with regard to this important matter, nor to anything else, and thus he even took control of our father right up to the moment when he was laid in earth. But *even that* has not yet been properly accomplished, as I explain below.

Clearly, there was the hand of Tommy in all this: he had pressured father to change his will to disinherit my family and me entirely. And what had Burnett got to say about it? He disingenuously asserted that he was 'only doing what he was told' in re-drafting father's two subsequent wills and that, due to professional confidentiality, he was not at liberty to discuss John's alleged recent decision to disinherit me! Considering the close relationships of all concerned it was outrageous that Burnett should hide behind such a notion. There was a clear conflict of interest. It is obvious I should have been informed of father's supposed change of heart, or Burnett should have stepped away from his involvement in re-drafting the wills. Further, I have always had a close and loving relationship with my father and it is inconceivable that *in his right mind* he would have elected to disinherit me without a word. In the last few years of his life he was increasingly infirm, confused, and deaf, and had complained to me several times that he was being bullied by Tommy.

In father's last will I am neither an executor nor beneficiary: Tommy is given these duties and privileges, together with Burnett as a joint executor and trustee. As for the witnesses, who were they? One was Tommy's coloured girlfriend, Carole—probably not someone father would have chosen if he had been mentally competent—and a certain Malik Tara.

Malik Tara was the son of the then downstairs neighbour, Michael Haag. If we give Carole the benefit of the doubt that she actually witnessed father signing everything away to

Tommy, the ink was hardly dry when Tommy rushed down to the basement flat and rang the bell. Malik Tara, a somewhat simple soul, appeared and was importuned to sign the will as if he were a witness present with the other two signatories, as required under the rules for witnessing wills. He later swore an affidavit to my solicitor that this was not true.

Events after the death of Renata Symonds

Mother died on 2 June 2007. After this event I decided to sell my flat at No 81. Therefore I had to clear the place of the furniture and I sent a fax to Tommy on 6 June:

> I wish to inform you that I intend to dispose of the remaining property of our late parents from my flat at 81 Belsize Lane. No doubt you will let me know if you have any observations on this matter.

He replied on 8 June in a letter obviously drafted by Burnett:

> The contents of the upper maisonette at 81 Belsize Lane has been left to me in our parent's wills and therefore please do not dispose of anything. Please allow me access according to the will and wishes of our parents for me to take possession of the aforementioned.
>
> Clive Burnett has written to [your solicitor] giving them information of the three wills and no doubt they will explain the situation to you in due course.

Having got into this formal way of corresponding, my response was as follows:

> I have received your illiterate fax of 8 June 2007 and am puzzled by your statement: 'The contents of the upper maisonette at 81 Belsize Lane has (*sic*) been left to me in our parent's (*sic*) wills…'

As you obviously are aware, when our parents moved into the flat it was fully furnished and nearly all the contents are in fact my property and never belonged to our parents. The only remaining items which belonged to them are their books, clothes, some kitchen equipment, the rug in the sitting room, and a few pieces of furniture, namely: the bureau desk in the sitting room, a few free-standing bookshelves, the small oak gate-legged table, the glass-fronted bookcase in the front bedroom, and one or two chairs.

On the other hand, you have already removed from the flat many items which clearly did belong to our parents. Many of these you removed even before they died. They include the following:

1. A large number of books from father's library in about twenty cardboard boxes
2. The entire stock of father's remaindered published and self-published works including many volumes of his plays and novels
3. All the pictures on the walls of the stairways, the common entrance hall, the front bedroom, and from the sitting room including a number of framed handwritten manuscripts from different regions of the world
4. The Buddha statuette and the carriage clock which were on the mantelpiece in the sitting room
5. All mother's musical instruments including one (possibly two) violins and bows and a viola and bow
6. The spice cabinet with the initials MS from inside my glass-fronted cabinet in the sitting room
7. The small two-drawer chest from the front bedroom
8. The VCR player from the rear bedroom
9. All of father's personal papers from the drawers of the desk and the above-mentioned chest in the front bedroom
10. The bulk of father's diaries

You are also in possession of mother's entire stock of jewellery, mainly expensive necklaces all or most of which were given to her by me over the years and which she mentioned several times she wished to leave to her granddaughter.

I am therefore proposing to place the remaining items belonging to our parents in storage until probate is granted and legal title to them has been established. I assume that neither you nor Burnett will object to this. I also expect you to do the same in respect of the items that you have removed. It is, after all, only fair that you should do so.

Unless and until probate is granted in respect of mother's and father's Wills, and the question of the executors and beneficiaries is properly determined, you must realise that you have no more claim to our parents' estate than I do.

This produced an angry response (Plate 13), drafted I suspect by Burnett, asserting Tommy's right to most of the contents of my flat, and ending somewhat incongruously with him sending his best wishes and signing himself formally as 'Tom Symonds'.

Terrorising the neighbours

From a short time before father died in September 2007, mother had been taken to live with Tommy; it was clear she was not coming back to live at No 81. So to prevent Tommy entering my flat and removing any more property, I had the locks changed. The front door of the house gave entry to the hall from which there was a door to the ground floor flat; this was occupied by an elderly couple. My flat was entered by a door on the first floor. A set of keys to the new locks on the street door was therefore provided to the ground floor tenants. Now, one fine day soon after this, Tommy turns up. His key to the front door doesn't work and no one answers the bell. So what does he do? Shrug his shoulders and go away? No. He shouts and bangs furiously at the front door. The poor people on the ground floor are alarmed and call the police. Police arrive and caution Tommy. This was the second time he was involved in a disturbance at this address and he was lucky not to get himself arrested.

10

CHALLENGING THE WILLS

I HAVE RELATED the above incidents in order to provide the context for understanding, as far as this may be possible, a gratuitous email from Tommy which arrived on 22 August 2005. It is quoted below in slightly shortened form. (Plate 14 shows the actual email from which I have redacted a few irrelevant abusive sentences.) It was the death knell for any kind of normal relationship between us:

> You have kept quiet about my dictionary because you are thoroughly nasty and a cheat. I am not prepared to do any deals with you. If my father told you to keep it this is pure chicanery on your part. You were not born yesterday and you know perfectly well that he is not capable of saying no to you. When my parents transferred £100,000 to you…you steadfastly held on to it for months after my mother had asked you to return it…
>
> You are one of the most evil and nasty people I have ever known or heard about. You have kept Renata as a slave for decades with you bullying nasty ways. You know all this and that she is afraid of you but you can only exist when you control and humiliate people. My mother only gave you that flat [12 Belsize Court] because she could not say no to you when you said you wanted it. You then proceeded in a scandalous way to chuck away £30,000 more than you needed, to refurbish it. It should have cost £10,000. You are despicable and flash with cash and your nastiness knows no bounds.
>
> When you decided to employ Carina you did so to only to bully my parents. You never discussed with them whether they were going to pay and they will not. Renata thought you

were doing it because you are kind. You are not kind but evil and nasty and even she knows this at last. We did not want to discuss the matter with you because there is never any discussion with you. You are only capable of bullying people and telling them what to do. Carole, whom you tried to throw out because she has a baby...has proved somebody my parents prefer having around their flat and is a lot cheaper. They would never have agreed to Carina if they had known you would expect them to pay...Don't you see dickhead, they are afraid of you but they are only agreeing because of the fear. You cannot re-negotiate a deal after the event. We will pay this time for this so keep your ugly proboscis out of our affairs.

When I tell people of what you did to Toby and how you have neglected him all these years they do not believe me and they think I am joking. You say you hope Toby does not treat me the way I treat my parents...You treat everybody in that mean controlling humiliating way, the only way you understand. Everybody who comes into contact with you hates and despises you. For you to have refused Toby to stay the night—I had to take him back to London at midnight. Outrageous. Renata should have told you to fuck off back to Japan there and then.

The reason you tell me your tenants left is because they don't want a shit for a landlord. Nobody leaves because a bailiff calls when your tenants were at work and some bailiffs' letters are sent. I had been using the address of No 12 for many years before you got your hands on it by chicanery and there was never a problem. Return my dictionary and the £500 you stole from me. You and your wife treated me worse than a dog when I visited you in Japan and you have never apologised for that or the time you ejected me from No 81. I might as well say you owe me £20,000 for all the mental stress you have caused in the family, and the analysis Toby needed because of his wicked Uncle.

One of your problems is that you are incapable of admitting a fault. Whenever Renata hints at something you don't agree with you put the phone down on her. You really are a shit... Somebody who has witnessed your behaviour recently described you as a baby throwing your toys out of the pram... The despicable way you carried on over the carpet you ought to be ashamed of yourself...bullying Renata over your rotten carpet saying that you would only allow her to have it if she went through the hassle of having the flat decorated. All this unpleasantness went on for months, but you always behave like that. You did it over Renata's 90th birthday and my father's 90th. You are like Hitler and Renata could not stand up to you and you knowing this kept her enslaved all these years.

You will have to pay for your sins in the next life make no mistake of that. To have given my name to the bailiffs or rather to Kernahans beggars belief to be so revengeful and nasty to your own brother. You are sick...You should deduct the £500 from their fees and send me the money. You could never admit a fault and thus you will remain a baby for the rest of your life.

I forwarded this email to a friend in Tokyo who had met Tommy; his reaction was:

It does appear that your brother is quite mad. I think that the time has come to completely ignore him. There is absolutely no point in justifying your own position because he is beyond reason and common sense.

What could induce a man to write in such an offensive way to anyone, let alone his own brother? This is the point at which, I am sorry to say, all the quotations at the beginning of this book are particularly apposite for Tommy's behaviour.

I shall not attempt a detailed refutation of this email where so much anger, hatred, and abuse are expressed, but some observations are needed.

All the problems Tommy alludes to reflect his own behaviour but they are projected onto me, for example, bullying and controlling our parents. Similarly, it is remarkable that I am blamed for Toby's alleged need for psychoanalysis, and in the next sentence that he says of me, 'One of your problems is that you are incapable of admitting a fault.'

A lot of it shows envy, such as his complaints over my acquisition of No 12. It is untrue that I asked our parents to give me this flat. On the contrary, I wanted them to use it for their own benefit and was content to inherit it, as they wished me to do, when the time came. As for what I spent to have it refurbished (he must have been told this by our parents) it was none of his business. The reference to £100,000 is also none of his business, but as mentioned above, I repaid it in full plus interest when father's court case was over. Tommy was worried that if this sum was not returned there would be less for him to inherit, since subsequent events showed he was already scheming to grab all our parents' money for himself! Further, it is significant that his concerns over the arrangements for caring for father while mother was in hospital, as detailed in Chapter 7, are centred on money rather than over what was best for our parents during that major crisis.

It is also interesting that he confesses, 'I had been using the address of No 12 for many years'—in other words, breaking the law.

While it might have had some value as an exercise to get in touch with his feelings, perhaps under the guidance of a psychotherapist, he seems to have used it merely as self-confirmation that he can do no wrong—it's always the other person's fault! In particular, with the reference to Hitler, it could be taken as an example of what C. G. Jung calls *pseudologia phantastica*, 'that form of hysteria which is characterized by a peculiar talent for believing in one's own lies.'[18]

---

18 The Collected Works of C. G. Jung, Vol 10, *Civilisation in Transition*, para 419. Routledge & Kegan Paul, 1964.

I also sent this email to mother. Her comment was, 'He's getting it off his chest.' So that's all right then. The apparent siding with Tommy I think is a reflection of prolonged 'grooming' of her to put me in a bad light. This is not just paranoia on my part but was observed by Vicki Harding and is mentioned in her Witness Statement quoted below. But our dear mother's inability to censure when it was needed did Tommy no good: he could never get things off his chest—they were always stuck there, like his pains.

On 5 October 2008 when the relationship between Tommy and me was at its lowest ebb and in my outrage at how he had treated our parents, I sent the following letter to him:

> You have destroyed our family.
>
> When our parents were dying, instead of cooperating with me to help them spend their last days in as comfortable and as pleasant a way as possible, for your own selfish ends you deliberately prevented them doing what they wished.
>
> I refer particularly to the last three weeks of Daddy's life. With great effort—and in spite of being obstructed at every step of the way by you—I managed to arrange for Daddy to be released from hospital and spend a few days in his own home in September 2006, to his enormous relief and joy. Alas, this was short-lived, for as soon as I had to leave to return to Japan you schemed to have him taken back in the middle of the night to the hospital. It was agreed with his GP, Dr Grun, that Daddy should be allowed to die at home and she had visited him the previous day. *Because of you he spent the last three weeks of his life in misery in hospital, begging to go home.* You didn't give a damn about Daddy's wishes. Even if you believed he needed readmission (which was not the case) after a few days when he had temporarily improved you could easily have arranged for new professional carers to be engaged, but you deliberately dragged your feet and had no intention of allowing him back home—*because the expense would have reduced your anticipated inheritance.*

In the case of Mummy, you were oblivious to, or deliberately trampled upon, her wishes: that she would have wanted to meet me in the last few months of her life. When I was in England in December 2006, having heard I was coming, you with malice aforethought took Mummy away from London on the ridiculous pretext of 'Mairead's mother's funeral' so that she was physically prevented from meeting me. Likewise, in February 2007, when I came upon you entering my flat at 81 Belsize Lane with Mummy you dragged her away. Why didn't you say: 'Yes, Mummy, you go in and talk to Gabriel and I'll return in an hour', or some such? *Because your pathological selfishness and hatred of me took precedence over everything else.* Likewise, you have despoiled her memory in ways too numerous to count. To give just one example: Mummy stated on several occasions that her jewellery, principally the necklaces which I gave her as birthday presents in the last ten years or so of her life, should be left to her granddaughter. Predictably, you grabbed these for yourself. If you had any spark of decency—which evidently you do not—you would arrange for these to be delivered forthwith to your niece, Erica.

It is also clear that for years you were scheming to have me disinherited from the small amount of money and other assets that Mummy and Daddy wished to leave *in equal shares to us both* as stated in their draft Wills of 2000 when they were in their right minds. What could be more normal and natural than that? But no. In your insane greed and egoism you couldn't stand this idea—*you wanted to have it all to yourself.* In Mummy's and Daddy's declining years they became more and more under your influence: by your almost daily visitations and haranguings you put me in a bad light and pressured them to rewrite their wills to exclude me.

You seemed to have forgotten, or you did not care, that you owed *everything* to Daddy. When as a neurotic whining schoolboy Daddy moved heaven and earth to help you[19]... Thereafter during all your adult life you sponged on our parents: they gave you the capital to buy a flat, various 'loans' such as £40,000 which was supposed to be repaid but probably never was, and numerous other sums: £10,000 here, £25,000 there, and many smaller sums which you screwed out of them. In 1999 alone, Daddy wrote cheques totalling £25,000 (possibly more) in your favour [Plate 15]. In addition, for three years he paid Toby's fees for Rugby School by standing order for around £1,500 per month.

What sort of man are you to have raided our elderly parents' savings in this way?

Yet, in spite of all the financial and other help which you received all your life from Mummy and Daddy and the extraordinary generosity with which they unfailingly treated you, when it came to the ends of their lives, *when they needed to spend their own money on themselves*, you subjected them to financial abuse and obstructed them.

Of course you will not agree with any of this but will argue until you are blue in the face that the earth is flat. And you will do this, as you have done practically all your life, because your insight into your own behaviour is *less than zero*.

By these actions you have ensured that you are permanently and irrevocably estranged from your own brother.

I sometimes wonder if, in the bottom of your black heart, you have any inkling that *what you did was wrong*. Somehow, I doubt it.

The only hope for you, as I see it, before you kick out your last tantrums in a health service geriatric home, is for you to go to our parents' graveside and on your knees beg their spirits for forgiveness.

Prescient letter

On 26 January 1985 father had written to me about the matter of making wills:

---

[19] Here I reiterate some of the history of Tommy's early life as set out in Chapter 2.

Those who die intestate (and have something in the way of worldly wealth to leave—blessed are the poor!) create unnecessary difficulties for their heirs...

The making of a will is a ticklish business. George Bernard Shaw, one for the cleverest of men, made a will 100 pages long; he left his considerable fortune to three institutions— he had no children and his wife predeceased him—the Royal Literary Fund, the Society of Authors, and the National Gallery of Ireland. But then he messed everything up by leaving a not inconsiderable portion of his vast wealth to the end that the spelling of English should be reformed on phonetic lines: 'rough' should be respelt 'ruff' and so on. No one knew how that could be put in practice, nor could the trustees or their experts agree among themselves on the matter.

A nearer example of the idiocy of will-makers is Aleister Crowley who made a will, which will when examined by a top lawyer of Lincoln's Inn—I employed him—he leant back in his chair and called it 'curious, he must have devised it himself', i.e., without guidance from his lawyer. Crowley died leaving little worldly wealth. He was living at the time in one room of a boarding house in Hastings, and was no sooner dead than the proprietor, an eccentric man with delusions of grandeur and other delusions who used to cross himself before approaching the Beast 666, crept into the room and stole his gold watch; so the most valuable object vanished; and when the loss was reported to the police a detective called on Lady Harris, wife of Sir Percy Harris, Bt., one of his executors, and asked her to hand it over. I should have said the most valuable tangible object. There were more valuable objects of an *intangible* kind, namely, Crowley's copyrights which at the time of his death in 1947 were worthless but which as the years rolled by became quite valuable. Now, to whom did he leave them? He wanted to leave them to his Order, the Order of Oriental Templars (*Ordo Templi Orientis*), which was dormant in Crowley's last years and at his death could be said to be defunct. So Crowley left his copyrights to his literary executor, John Symonds, author of an illustrated novel called *William Waste*, for him to hand over *on demand* to the Grand Treasurer General of the non-existent order, one Karl Germer of New York, the biggest ass in the whole of Christendom—no, I mustn't exaggerate—*one* of the biggest asses—who after Crowley's death wore the Master's magic ring, contemplated a pile of Crowley's magic books, and called himself the Supreme and Holy King of the Order of Oriental Templars. And he never asked me to hand over the copyrights, and I therefore never handed them over; so they remained, and still remain, with me.

But this hasn't stopped various demented persons in the United States, Switzerland, Brazil, and elsewhere from obtaining a copy of Crowley's will from Somerset House, misinterpreting it, and calling themselves Heads of the Order of Oriental Templars, without any charter to prove it, and forthwith publishing the *opera* of Crowley without any reference to me at all. Now, all this could have been avoided had Crowley clearly left his copyrights to me.

I have little of value to leave with the exception of my copyrights which today aren't worth much but which I believe will be of value in the future, perhaps of considerable value, hopefully before I'm called away to heaven. That is, the copyrights of my published—almost all of them have reverted to me—and unpublished works, including of course my diaries, which, years ago, Dr Eric Dingwall, the Keeper of the 'cupboard' books in the British Museum Library (now the National Library)—you met him, do you remember?—asked me to leave to the Museum.

I shall leave everything to you and your brother to be divided equally between you [emphasis added]. If my plays get going that could bring in yearly a great deal of money; this would produce a demand for the republication of my novels. My diaries are of considerable interest, although I say it myself. Copyright lasts till fifty years after the death of the author and in the case of works not published in the author's lifetime, from fifty years from the date of publication.

Crowley's will was divided into two parts, his tangible goods, and his copyrights. The first part was proved shortly after his death. The copyright part was just left, and years later I sought and obtained probate on it, and the value of the copyrights was pitched very low, about £100 I think, so the state got nothing from Crowley's will and I got only a small part of what I should have got because of unscrupulous publishers, mainly in the US.

Copyright of the printed word is in itself a difficult business. Only recently has it been internationally sorted out. Japan only recognised copyright of books published since 1970; so they translate and issue anything they like before that date without paying the authors anything.

I shall leave, unless you think otherwise, that portrait of me by Stella Schmolle[20] to the National Portrait Gallery; I think they would accept it, especially if my reputation has begun to rise at my decease, or if they don't, to the Humanities Research Center of the University of Texas at Austin, where most of my MSS are; they would certainly take it.

My diaries are a bit of a problem. I don't want them to be shown to anyone who may take it into his or her head to write a biography of me. *Their publication in whole or in part by some good press and under the editorship of some scholarly person could produce an income for you and Tommy.* [Emphasis added.]

How to make lawyers rich

After the deaths of our parents I was left with a difficult situation: it was obvious that their last wills had been re-written at Tommy's

---

20 Stella Schmolle was an artist who lived next door to our parents when they were at 66 Lyncroft Mansions. She was known for the paintings she produced while conscripted into the Auxiliary Territorial Service during World War II and for her post-war portrait paintings. She made a fine oil portrait of John Symonds in his fifties which he gave to Tommy.

direction with the collusion of the man who was still acting as my accountant, Clive Burnett. Tommy then pressured our parents to sign these false wills when they were enfeebled by old age and unable to resist him, let alone understand the amended contents.

I therefore sought legal advice about having the wills set aside. As a first step a *caveat* was placed upon them; it is still in being. This means that probate cannot be granted and no one can act on the provisions of the wills.

Before taking further steps I attempted to negotiate with Tommy through Burnett. Not all this correspondence has been preserved, but I have a copy of the proposals I sent him on 22 December 2008:

> You drafted wills for John and Renata Symonds in 2000. In these wills they stated their wishes that their estates were to be left *in equal shares* to Thomas and me. You have been asked more than once whether these wills were executed, and if not, why not, but you have refused to answer these and related questions. The later wills which my parents signed I believe are invalid: Renata's will of March 2007 was signed a mere three months before her death when she was in an advanced stage of senility with severe memory loss and totally under Thomas's control. John's will of May 2005 was signed at a time when he was suffering from confusion and hearing impairment; in addition, this will was improperly witnessed. It is also clear that the drafting and alleged execution of these wills were orchestrated and manipulated by Thomas to try to achieve his selfish ends of excluding me and grabbing everything for himself, and that you colluded in this.
>
> At the time in question I was one of your paying clients and regarded you as a 'family friend' who could be relied upon to 'see fair play' in the serious dispute that was developing between Thomas and me. The confidence which I had in your objectivity and fairness I realised—too late—was misplaced. When I raised my concerns that Thomas was seeking to influence our parents and might remove

their assets before probates were granted, you assured me, falsely as it turned out, that you would not allow it. Further, when you claimed that John wanted to change his will with new instructions which apparently required 'many hours of discussion'—an absurd and false claim[21]—for you to hide behind the notion of professional confidentiality as a reason not to let me know something was afoot, is disingenuous. Your unprofessional behaviour over this and your siding with Thomas are disgraceful.

In addition, in spite of being repeatedly asked by my solicitor about the existence of other wills of John and Renata, you have engaged in delaying tactics and obstruction to avoid answering this question.

Furthermore, it seems to me improper that while Renata was still living independently you gained control of her savings of around £110,000, putting them into your Client Account and have refused to answer my concerns about this transaction. I should be interested to know where this money is now, or whether Renata 'gave' it to Thomas before she died. No doubt you will still refuse to say unless I obtain a court order to compel you to do so. This makes me wonder whether you have something to hide.

All this bears on the matter of achieving a settlement with Thomas, and you should be aware that what I require is as follows:

1. The basis for resolving the dispute over our parents' wills should be the draft wills of 2000 when they were in reasonably good health, in their right minds, and not subject to undue influence.

---

[21] If John Symonds in his right mind wanted to change his will all he needed to do was to say to Burnett: 'I've decided to disinherit Gabriel and leave everything to Thomas. Please re-draft my will accordingly.' Why were 'many hours of discussion' needed? And where are Burnett's Attendance Notes on these discussions? In any case, in the last two or three years of John's life it was impossible to have a conversation with him beyond a few minutes because of his deafness and confusion.

2. This means, in particular, that the copyrights in John's and Renata's published and unpublished works should be shared equally between Thomas and me.
3. There should be equal access to John's diaries. Their eventual disposal should be subject to arbitration, if necessary, and any profits arising from their sale should be shared equally.
4. Renata's musical instruments and the Buddha statuette should pass to me, and the spice cabinet with the initials MS should pass to my wife, Masumi Symonds. Thomas would keep the French clock and he may keep the pictures and other chattels, except as below, which he has already removed from 81 Belsize Lane.
5. I wish to have three copies from as many of the individual twenty-six plays that are in Thomas's possession, as well as a few copies of the remaindered sets of his novels, etc.
6. Although it is not in the will, Renata mentioned a number of times that her jewellery, mainly necklaces of pearls and semi-precious stones which I gave her as birthday presents in the last decade or so of her life, should pass to her grand-daughter, Erica.
7. From Renata's cash assets I should be reimbursed the cost of the carers who briefly looked after John in September 2006 (about £1,000) and the Service Charges at 81 Belsize Lane due in January 2007 and pro-rata till May 2007 which Renata would have paid (about £3,666) had Thomas not prevented her from doing so.
8. The residue of about £110,000 which was in the Woolwich Guernsey account and subsequently transferred to your Client Account should be divided equally between Thomas and me, net of funeral expenses.
9. It must be understood that nearly all the contents of the flat at 81 Belsize Lane are my property and it is therefore fraudulent for Thomas to claim he is entitled to them. The few remaining objects which did belong to our parents are of no commercial value.

10. The following property of mine which Thomas unlawfully removed from 81 Belsize Lane must be returned to me:
    a) The portrait of Renata by Michael Taylor
    b) Various personal papers
    c) Two volumes of the Oxford Junior Encyclopaedia (*The Universe* and *Law and Order*) and other books

This proposal was ignored.

Although I then went to considerable trouble and expense consulting solicitors and learned Counsel about challenging my parents' wills, I was advised of their opinion that the chance of success was less than 50 per cent, and therefore I could not be recommended to proceed. This was mainly because of the Attendance Note referred to above: at its face value it seemed my mother was clear in her mind that she wanted to cut me out of her will, and it would probably be difficult to persuade a judge otherwise. But even if my father's last two wills were set aside, his estate would pass to my mother since she survived him. It was not as if millions of pounds were at stake; the cash amount involved was relatively small—something slightly in excess of £100,000. I therefore decided it was not worthwhile, even though a matter of principle was involved, to pursue challenging the wills.

Recovering my stolen property was another matter. My next step, therefore, was to instruct my solicitors to bring an action against Tommy for theft. A writ was served on him and in due course a date was set for the hearing. I was represented by my solicitors and Tommy, assisted by his 'litigation friend', Burnett, was the defendant.

The Particulars of Claim were that Thomas J Symonds without lawful authority had removed from my flat at 81 Belsize Lane various property belonging to me including, and in particular, the portrait of my mother by Michael Taylor that I had had commissioned, and various books and personal papers. I had paid £8,250 for the portrait but the other goods were of sentimental value only.

The document (13 February 2009) setting out my claim, in part reads as follows:

> (1) The delivery up forthwith of the Claimant's Goods, and damages consequent upon the wrongful interference with the same by their detention;
> (2) Alternatively, damages;
> (3) Interest pursuant to Section 35A of the Supreme Court Act 1981 or as the Court may consider just;
> (4) Such further or other relief as the Court shall consider just; and
> (5) Costs

However, since the commercial value of my property was relatively low, the judge refused to hear the case because he decided that it should be moved to the Small Claims Court—for which I would have to attend in person. So much for my solicitors: they should have known this would happen. A date was then set for a Small Claims hearing but it was too difficult for me to leave my busy single-handed practice in Tokyo to travel to London. In any case, Tommy might well have sought an adjournment on some pretext, knowing that I could not absent myself from Japan for more than a short time. I therefore withdrew my claim and the case lapsed, but the *caveats* have remained in force.

Then I received on 20 December 2009 a proposal from Burnett for an out-of-court settlement:

> It's been a long time since we last talked and I thought at this time of year we could try to settle our differences. Although you withdrew your claim against Tom, perhaps we can still achieve the main part of the result you wanted, without having to spend tens of thousands of pounds in legal & Court fees.

I have been speaking with Tom who would also like to resolve the issues at hand and therefore, with his agreement, I would like to suggest the following:

1) Ownership of the copyrights, works, manuscripts and all the diaries of the late John Symonds pass to Tom Symonds, so that the missing diaries are returned to Tom
2) All other assets (save those listed below) contained in the Wills of John & Renata Symonds pass to Tom Symonds
3) The painting of Renata Symonds is returned to Gabriel Symonds
4) Gabriel Symonds retains ownership of 'the dictionary'
5) All disputes regarding the other missing contents of the flat at 81 Belsize Lane are closed and no action is taken by either party against the other

The offer is conditional upon the caveats lodged by you against the two Wills held in probate being lifted. I trust you will now consider this proposal seriously so that we can all move forward.

With best wishes for Christmas…[!]

In other words, I would merely have my stolen property returned and Tommy would get everything else. (The *Dictionary*, as already explained, belonged to me anyway.) This proposal amounted to an admission that my portrait had been removed in anticipation of using it as a kind of hostage in case Tommy might need it for such purpose. And Burnett's vaunted professional integrity, about which he never tired of boasting, is seen for what it is: collusion with an illegal act of his client and friend, Tommy, in a clear conflict of interest with another client, myself.

Although I used rather different words, my reaction to this contemptible proposal was the same as that in Arkell v. Pressdram. This was the final response of the publishers of

Private Eye (the British satirical magazine) when being sued by a Mr James Arkell for libel. It consisted of only two words, the first of which begins with 'F', and the second with 'O'.

I replied (22 December 2009) to Burnett as follows:

> You make no reference to my refutation of Thomas's alleged justification for having taken the portrait. I repeat that I believe you are well aware that a) the portrait was commissioned and paid for by me, and therefore b) it is and always has been my property and was not Renata's to give away, and c) if Renata allegedly 'gave' it to Thomas she did so in error, being not in her right mind because she was at that time suffering from confusion and marked memory loss. In this connection it is significant that at no time did Thomas contact me to confirm whether I had given the portrait to Renata.
>
> The portrait was removed from my flat while both John and Renata were alive, probably in the early part of 2006. The question of ownership of the portrait is, therefore, entirely separate from the question of determination of the wills.
>
> Thomas is using the portrait to try to obtain unfair concessions from me over the wills. Knowing this fact, it is disgraceful that you appear to be colluding with Thomas in his machinations to disinherit me.
>
> As for the *Dictionary*, it is unclear on what basis Thomas is offering to let me retain ownership of it, since these two volumes were given to me by John according to a letter (which I have previously quoted to you) which he sent me in 1990.
>
> I repeat, yet again, that Thomas must immediately and unconditionally return the portrait to me, and I request your help in persuading him to do this.
>
> That apart, I ask you, now for the fourth time, to respond to my counter-proposals for settling the question of the wills.

To this, likewise, Burnett did not favour me with a reply.

Witness statements

In 2010, when I started legal proceedings against Tommy to recover my stolen property, part of the documentation was two Witness Statements. I include them here since they give other people's views on the matter. One is that of Vicki Harding (20 February 2010) which is entitled 'Mental State of Renata Symonds'. The emphases are in the original:

> I have been a close friend of John and Renata Symonds for thirty years, visiting them regularly, especially in recent years when they were in declining physical health. At no time was I aware of any suggestion either from John or Renata that they were displeased with or upset about Gabriel; on the contrary, they always spoke with pleasure of their family in Japan and often expressed a wish to go there again even when John's physical health made it impossible. Renata would not have gone without John while he was alive, and in later years she was concerned about her angina too. *However, on two or three occasions between January and March 2007 when I was able to meet Renata alone, she told me that she wished to move to Japan (where Gabriel and his family live) as she wanted to get away from Thomas's influence.*
>
> It is inconceivable to me that at any time in recent years Renata would have initiated a major change in her will compared with her draft will of 2000. On about six occasions *between November 2006 and May 2007* when I reminded her *of how John had apparently been influenced in rewrite his will to leave everything to Thomas and nothing to Gabriel, and when I raised my suspicions that she may have been pressured by Thomas to rewrite her own will similarly, without remembering that she had done so,* she was every time horrified: 'But that's despicable, he can't do that, what can we do? We must call the police!' (Due to her failing memory, each time this matter arose it was for her as if for the first time.)
>
> In my opinion, *for about the last two years of her life Renata showed symptoms of severe short-term memory loss and marked*

confusion. She did not have the concentration or mental capacity to draft a will such as the one she has apparently signed, or to be able to read it through and understand it fully.

On the other hand, *as I witnessed on a number of occasions*, Thomas was well used to haranguing his parents until they gave him what he wanted. John told me of his rift with Thomas about five years ago over his frequent demands for money with promises of returning it that Thomas was unconcerned about fulfilling and rarely did. It was plain to me that John and Renata found it very difficult to resist Thomas, and it was many years after John first told me of his feelings about Thomas before he acted on them. He had always said he felt responsible as a father for Thomas, and thus was prepared *in large measure* to put up with his bad behaviour and look at his good points.

I believe that Thomas himself was instrumental in drafting the alleged wills of his parents that excluded his brother as an equal beneficiary, that neither his father nor mother had any independent part in conceiving or writing them, and that they were both tricked and would not have signed them if they were fully aware of the contents. I further believe, from my observations over three decades, that Renata was badgered by Thomas into signing these later wills in Thomas's presence, *and that she did not understand the implications of what she was doing* even if the contents had been summarised for her. She was considerably confused and ill in the few months before her death, and I feel asking her to do this would have been cruel in the extreme, as well as not fulfilling her previously stated wishes.

Finally, considering how much her daughter-in-law, Masumi Symonds, and her grandchildren, meant to her, I find it *unbelievable* that Renata in her right mind would have wished the only other beneficiary (as I understand is mentioned in Renata's alleged last will) to be Maureen

McLean, the mother of Thomas's son Toby, and would have entirely excluded Gabriel and his side of the family.

There is an appendix to this Witness Statement which gives further insight into the family relationships:

Thomas's hatred for his brother

In early 2006 one of John's plays [*The Poison Maker*] was being performed at a local theatre which I attended with Renata. I went home with her afterwards to 81 Belsize Lane. While I was there, Thomas rang up and I asked to speak to him to tell him how much I had enjoyed the play. However, before I could do so he launched into a diatribe of 'how awful' his brother Gabriel was, 'like Hitler' etc. I refused to get drawn into this and handed the telephone back to Renata,

With great effort I managed to maintain good relations with Thomas until after his father's funeral. I had tried to help him over the funeral arrangements, for instance, by finding names and phone numbers of John's old friends, checking out venues for holding the wake, and offering to help on the day. In spite of this, Thomas's plotting to prevent Gabriel's side of the family attending was the final straw which led to the breakdown of our relationship. I ignored his provocations as much as possible, but when he repeatedly lied in front of me to his mother and others, and deliberately procrastinated over the date of the funeral, I refused to condone his behaviour and he became incensed. In the event, he gave Gabriel just three days' notice of the funeral which made it impossible for people to come from Japan, to say nothing of the difficulty it caused me and my partner, Robert. Subsequently, he expressed completely unjustified anger and criticism towards Gabriel and his wife for not coming.

Thomas's hostility for his brother extended even to those he perceived as being 'on Gabriel's side', in particular, to me, as happened after the inevitable breakdown in our relationship after John's funeral.

- In May 2007, during Renata's final hospital admission when I would visit her with Robert, sometimes we would bump into Thomas on the ward. Without regard for anyone else within earshot, he was abusive to our faces, accusing me of being 'The Enemy' and calling Robert 'Dickhead'. This was obviously so unpleasant and distressing to Renata that we tried not to visit when there was a risk Thomas would be there.
- I visited Renata with Gabriel on one day in mid-May 2007 when he came over from Japan to visit her as she was then close to the end of her life. Gabriel felt it necessary to go to the extraordinary length of engaging the services of a professional bodyguard to keep Thomas at bay, so we could visit Renata without risking a confrontation at the bedside if he turned up at the same time. In the event, this proved a wise and necessary precaution.

<u>'Coaching' of Renata by Thomas</u>

It was during the period immediately after Renata was in hospital with a broken hip in July 2005 that it became clear Thomas was coaching his mother in what to do and say for his own ends. For example, during this family emergency, I was involved in helping to arrange live-in carers for John, who at that stage was incapable of living independently. However, any discussion I had with Renata about carers for John was met by statements that she did not like the proposed person involved (a professional carer found by Gabriel at short notice), even though she had never met her, and that she was too expensive, even though her fees were modest. It was clear that these negative views were planted in his mother's mind by Thomas once the deterioration in her memory meant this was possible: he didn't like the fact that the carer had been arranged by Gabriel and that she cost anything at all. It was disgracefully obvious that Thomas's over-riding motive was to prevent his parents spending their own money on professional carers so that his anticipated 'inheritance' would not thereby be diminished.

Thomas's shocking behaviour towards his dying father

When John became bedridden in August 2006, his GP, Dr Lucia Grun, told me she had said to Thomas, 'If it were my parents I would think it worth spending some money to make their lives more comfortable and do what they wanted,' and Thomas had replied that he wanted to avoid spending 'his inheritance' on carers because 'It's my money!'

John returned home that night and spent the following four days at home, Gabriel in the meantime having returned to Japan. I visited daily while John was at home and observed the following:

- The carers told me they slept together upstairs and barricaded the door if Thomas was around. They said not only had Thomas been rude and abusive to them, but he had gone into their room without asking, to harangue them and interfere with their belongings.
- On 27th September Thomas engineered that John was taken back to hospital against everyone's wishes, especially including John's, and against the advice of the GP who had visited earlier in the day and agreed that John should be allowed to die at home. I also had visited John earlier that day and while I was there Thomas turned up. I was present during a conversation in which Thomas repeatedly asked Renata to tell him his (Thomas's) telephone number to make sure she had not forgotten it. Then he said to his mother, 'You will call me this evening when Daddy wants something won't you.' This was repeated over and over again. Thomas was cuddling her, which was unusual in front of me, and both were smiling and looked conspiratorial. I

felt uncomfortable in Thomas's presence and with this behaviour, and didn't understand it at the time. When the neighbour downstairs (Michael Haag) rang me at home later to say that Thomas had managed to get an ambulance to take John back to hospital, he told me that Thomas 'looked like the cat that got the cream'. It was then that it dawned on me how Thomas had got Renata to panic and call him for help in the middle of the night so that an ambulance was called and the carers kept out of the way—they were upstairs with the door shut as they had been made frightened of Thomas. They would go down to check on John from time to time, but unfortunately they hadn't heard the ambulance men coming. Michael Haag, however, related to me later that he questioned the ambulance men and Renata, and tried to reason with them to leave John at home, but while he went upstairs to fetch the carers whom he found in their attic room, John was taken away. He said Renata was in a daze and by this time Thomas had arrived and was directing events.

- When John was in hospital the carers (engaged by Gabriel) promptly left; they had had enough of Thomas's rudeness and intimidating behaviour. So, there was John back in the Royal Free Hospital—bed bound, physically helpless, and at the terminal stage of his life. But he was alert enough to say what he wanted: to go home! This he repeated endlessly to anyone who visited him—to Renata, his grandchildren, the Haags, and me. The poor man constantly begged to go home.
- Now, his home had been organised (to the satisfaction of the hospital authorities) so that he could be there if there was day and night professional help: a special bed had been installed, incontinent pants had been delivered in quantity, a ripple mattress (to prevent bedsores) had been provided, etc. Obviously, this kind of nursing help could not be provided by the local authority—it would

need to be paid for privately. Where would the money come from for this emergency? From John and Renata's savings account with the Woolwich Guernsey. I was informed that they had well in excess of £100,000 for this very purpose. So why couldn't new professional carers be promptly engaged from one of the many private agencies? Because Thomas didn't allow it. He didn't want his 'inheritance' to be reduced. He paid lip-service to the idea of engaging private carers, but dragged his feet. With his domineering personality, with Renata's mental and physical feebleness, and with Gabriel being back in Japan, there was no way anyone could stand up to Thomas to allow his dying father to be nursed at home. And so, three weeks later, he died in the hospital.

[Signed]

The other Witness Statement is Michael Haag's (3 February 2010):

1) I have lived at 81A Belsize Lane, London NW3, since 1996 where I became friends with my upstairs neighbours John and Renata Symonds at 81 Belsize Lane and remained so until their deaths (John age 92 in 2006; Renata age 93 in 2007). We often visited one another, including many times when my wife and I would be invited upstairs for dinner. We were entrusted with the Symonds' flat keys, and as they got older my wife and I frequently helped them up the stairs with their shopping and assisted them in various ways as they became progressively more weak, forgetful, and confused. I also got to know John and Renata Symonds' two sons, Gabriel and Thomas.

2) Gabriel Symonds commissioned for himself as a keepsake a portrait of his mother Renata Symonds by the well known painter Michael Taylor which was completed in 2004.

I always understood that Gabriel intended to take the portrait with him to Japan, where he lives and has a medical practice. But meanwhile he allowed the painting to remain in London, first at the request of Michael Taylor who exhibited at the Royal Society of Portrait Painters' annual exhibition in May 2005.

3) Michael Taylor's painting marvellously captures Renata Symonds' intelligence, charm and good humour, and it is not surprising that it was selected, along with another portrait of Michael Taylor's, of the writer P D James, to be shown at the Geffrye Museum in London from October 2007 as part of a major exhibition of twentieth century urban domestic interiors. Accordingly, Gabriel continued to allow the painting to remain at his parents' flat.

4) I recall that on a visit to London in 2006, at time when his father John Symonds was approaching death, Gabriel discovered that the portrait of his mother was missing from his parents' flat. His brother Thomas admitted that he had it in his possession. John Symonds died on 21 October 2006; Renata died on 2 June 2007. The Geffrye Museum exhibition was set for 16 October 2007, but Thomas refused to allow the painting to be shown, claiming that it was his, and that it had been given him by his mother Renata.

5) Thomas Symonds' claim to own the portrait of his mother flies against everything I know about the painting and Gabriel's intentions for it. I do not believe that Renata Symonds gave the painting to Thomas. For a start, she did not own the painting; Gabriel did. Moreover, any clam that Renata Symonds did give the painting to Thomas is vitiated by the fact that she had begun to suffer serious memory loss from July 2005 when she went to hospital with a broken hip. She was confused and forgetful throughout the last two years of her life, even to the extent of forgetting to eat, and was not capable of making a responsible decision.

6) I believe that the facts in the witness statement are true.

[Signed]

I regret to record that Michael Haag died in January 2020.

***

As explained above it was impractical for me to proceed with this litigation, and the situation thus appeared to be at a stalemate. But then there was a new development which I describe in the following chapter.

11
NEGLECTED GRAVE

AFTER I CONDUCTED the memorial service for mother in 2008 I did not have occasion to visit London again until 2014, at which time I went to pay my respects at our parents' grave in Highgate Cemetery. But I was shocked to see the grave was in a neglected state. There was no gravestone—just the earth covered with grass and weeds, though someone had recently left some cut flowers—but there were two small temporary wooden crosses which had been place asymmetrically: one showed father's name and dates, the other, just mother's name.

When someone is buried a period of two to three years needs to elapse to allow the ground to settle before a stone memorial can be emplaced, so after this time why hadn't Tommy organised it?

I soon discovered the reason: there is a rule that until probate is granted on the will of the second-deceased (both parents are in the same grave) the grave technically belongs to our mother, so that it is impermissible for anyone to arrange for a stone memorial to be erected.

Although by that time Tommy and I were estranged, it was so distressing to see the neglected state of the grave that I couldn't let the matter rest. But in order to avoid the unpleasantness of direct communication with Tommy, I instructed a new solicitor to write (1 September 2014) to him:

> We are informed that our client recently visited your parents' grave in Highgate Cemetery and was shocked to find it in a neglected state. There are only two temporary wooden crosses and no memorial has been erected.

Our client can only assume that the reason for this is that you have been unable to proceed with the administration of your late mother's estate due to the caveat lodged by our client.

Our client finds this neglect of the graves distressing and this has prompted him to take steps to address the current unhappy state of affairs and the impasse that has been reached.

It is our client's case that the wills made by your late father in 2005 and that made by your mother in 2007 were invalid having been made with undue influence being exerted upon them by you but additionally in the case of your father's will as it was improperly witnessed (one witness not being present when your father signed it). We understand that your parents drafted wills in 2000 when they were in reasonable health and had the requisite mental capacity and in which they expressed a wish that their estates should be left to you both in equal shares.

We are instructed that Mr Clive Burnett, the second named substitute executor in the disputed will of your late mother, contacted our client and proposed that if he withdraw the caveat you would return to our client the portrait of your late mother by the artist Michael Taylor. It is our client's case that this portrait belonged to him and that you unlawfully removed the same from his flat 81 Belsize Lane in or around 2006. Mr Burnett also proposed that you would relinquish your claim to a first edition of Samuel Johnson's *Dictionary*. Again it is our client's case that he was the rightful owner of this, it having been gifted to him by your late father in 1990. It follows that Mr Burnett was simply proposing to return to our client property which already belonged to him but you would retain the residue of your parents' estates including the sum of approximately £110,000 (cash assets) and the ownership of the copyrights in your parents' published and unpublished works.

Our client did make a counter proposal to Mr Burnett based on the provisions of the wills drafted in 2000 but tells us that he received no response from you or Mr Burnett.

In order to now resolve matters our client proposes the following:-

1. You accept that the wills made by your parents in 2005 and 2007 are invalid.
2. If the wills your parents had intended to make in 2000 were executed by them that:
(a) Mr Burnett renounces his executorship thereof,
(b) That application is made for a grant of probate in respect of your mother's will in the joint names and you and our client.
3. You and our client apply to be the joint statutory owners of the exclusive rights of burial in respect of your parents' grave.
4. Arrangements are made for a memorial to be erected in a form jointly agreed by you and our client.
5. The aforementioned portrait of your mother to be returned to our client.
6. The residue of the aforementioned £110,000.00 after deduction costs of the memorial be divided equally between you and our client.
7. That you and our client have equal authority to dispose of the copyrights of your parents published and unpublished works and to share any profits arising therefrom.
8. Our client has access to your father's diaries for a reasonable period of time after which they would be offered for sale to the British Library (as an expressed wish in your father's will) and that you should share equally any profit arising therefrom.
9. Our client should be given copies of your father's published and self-published works as there are or were many copies of the same in your possession.
10. Our client has in the last few years received a number of enquiries from publishers who are interested in republishing

several of your father's works. This is a matter from which you could both potentially benefit but obviously the question of the ownership of the copyrights needs to be resolved first. We would ask you and Mr Burnett to refrain from contacting our client directly in respect of any negotiations relating to the resolution of the issues between you and our client. Any communications with our client should come through us.

Some of the correspondence after that is missing, but after months-long delays on Tommy's side a counter-proposal was received from him which, *under the circumstances*, was not unreasonable. The main points were that in return for lifting the caveats Tommy would pay me £25,000, I would yield up all of our father's diaries in my possession, and he would allow me to gain title to the copyrights of two works of our parents. One was a charming children's book, *The Isle of Cats*. It was first published in 1955 and there was a second edition in 1979. It's about me and a cat we used to have called Uncle Tom (!):

> It all began when Gabriel decided that he wouldn't go to school. Instead, he went with his cat, Uncle Tom, on a flying visit to the mysterious Isle of Cats. There he was shown around by the cat mayor, and discovered a topsy-turvy country of cat soldiers, wrestlers, orphans, cooks, and frustrated inventors. Many other surprises were in store before Gabriel and Uncle Tom made their way home again, just in time for tea.
> John Symonds's hilarious story is delightfully illustrated by Gerard Hoffnung at his most witty and inventive.

The other work was our mother's unpublished *Midlife: Problems and Solutions*. There was only a bound typescript which I had brought to Japan together with some of the other books belonging to our parents. Tommy wanted a photocopy of the *Midlife* typescript *and five copies of the printed book* if it were published! I was particularly keen to have title to the copyright of this work because an interest had been shown in it by the distinguished house of Routledge, formerly Routledge & Kegan Paul, the publishers of the English translation of the Collected Works of C. G. Jung. This would have been a great posthumous honour for my mother. The other important clause was that if the caveats were lifted, Tommy would without delay arrange for a stone memorial to be erected with wording on the headstone to be agreed between us.

This looked promising, but in my experience few things to do with Tommy are straightforward. In the middle of the negotiations he demanded that I tell him which years of father's diaries I had. Why did he do that? He knew the years he already had—the bulk of them—and he could have worked out those years that he believed were missing from his stockpile. So he could easily have told me which volumes he was expecting, or he could just have waited till he received those which were in my possession since I gave an undertaking that all those I had would be held by my solicitor until the matter was settled. But Tommy was insistent, so I told him: they were those of the years 1993, 1996, 1997, 1999, 2000, and 2001.

This immediately threw a spanner in the works that was to jeopardise the whole deal. Some diaries were missing! He demanded that I produce those from the years 1947–54 or reveal their whereabouts. He claimed that if I was not secretly keeping them, then Vicki, Michael Haag, or my daughter had made off with them! Just as Tommy had been frantic to get his hands on the few diaries I had managed to keep out of his clutches at the difficult time of our father's death, now his obsession to obtain 'all' the diaries was renewed to the point where he appeared to be unhinged.

I think these diaries never existed and he was simply mistaken about them. One reason was that I started keeping a daily journal myself in 1955 when I was 10 years old. I found in the local stationery shop a Collin's page-a-day diary with a hardback red cover which I bought with my pocket money, and I have kept a diary ever since. Inspired by me, father also started this practice in 1955, as did Tommy himself.

Furthermore, I found Tommy's whole behaviour over the alleged missing years' diaries was devious. I suspect he changed his mind because he could not stand the thought of giving me any money at all, and he used the idea of the non-production of these alleged volumes as an excuse to withdraw his offer of the £25,000—for that is what he did.

At first, with the prospect of Routledge publishing *Midlife* (which they wouldn't do in any case unless I was the legal copyright holder), I thought I would forgo the money and complete the agreement otherwise. That would have meant at least that our parents would finally get a decent burial and I would have my stolen property returned. And Tommy would get everything else.

Unfortunately, however, *Midlife* was turned down by Routledge. So I published it myself, copyright the estate of Renata Symonds. It is a fine scholarly, yet accessible work. I edited the text, added an Introduction, and wrote a blurb for the back cover:

> This book is the distillation of the professional wisdom of Renata Symonds (1913 – 2007), a London-based Jungian psychotherapist.
>
> She deals with the perennial problems of humankind that may particularly become evident at the threshold of the second half of life: finding meaning in one's existence; facing conflicts in work and marriage; dealing with depression, loneliness, and sexuality; and fear of death.
>
> These great themes are explored from the perspective of the writer's experience in helping people become aware of the unconscious aspects of their problems, especially through dream analysis. Many cases are described of how clients in this way—rather than by resorting to medical drugs to suppress symptoms—make real progress not only in resolving their difficulties but also in achieving inner growth.
>
> No dry treatise or self-help book—how to recognise if you're going through a midlife crisis and what to do about

it—Renata Symonds speaks with warmth and enthusiasm of her approach to her clients' difficulties. The text is enriched by references to Jung and Freud and contains many literary and mythological allusions.

This book will be of interest to the general reader with a basic knowledge of Jung's ideas, as well as to those undergoing or contemplating psychotherapy.

I also included two other works by Renata Symonds: *The Magic Mirror*, a lecture given at the Westminster Pastoral Foundation in 1981, and a talk, *Patterns and Quality of Leadership*, probably given in the late 1970s for the then Inner London Education Authority, Westminster Area Youth Office. (Copyright: Westminster Pastoral Foundation and the estate of Renata Symonds, respectively.)

Having done this, there remained little incentive for me to proceed with the agreement without a monetary consideration'. As for the grave, I managed to improve it by having a new temporary wooden cross erected (Plate 16) which was permissible, and in doing this I received the kind assistance of the staff at Highgate Cemetery. A plaque was affixed, properly worded:

> In Loving Memory of
> JOHN SYMONDS
> Author and Dramatist
> 1914 – 2006
> and
> RENATA SYMONDS
> Psychotherapist
> 1913 – 2007

Predictably, Tommy didn't like it. On 11 March 2018 he wrote to me directly: 'I intend to take down an ugly cross that recently appeared on our parents' grave.' To this needless provocation I felt obliged to reply:

> I would advise against interfering with our parents' grave until you have the authority to do so consequent upon my removal of the caveats. As you know, father was conversant with the Black Arts, and if in the meantime you remove the cross, for certain a Curse will fall upon you!

Negotiations then stalled, but on 1 November 2017 I wrote to him again, this time in anger:

> It is utterly disgraceful that you have ignored all conciliatory approaches to cooperate with me so that our parents can at last be decently buried.
>
> You abused our parents during their lifetimes; you are showing contempt for them after their deaths.
>
> The only reason I tried to negotiate with you is because of your low meanness in leaving our parents' grave neglected—which I only discovered in 2014. It is perfectly clear that either you didn't care whether a memorial was emplaced, so you did nothing about it, or, if you had enquired about a memorial you would soon have been informed this is not allowed until probate has been granted. But probate could not be granted because there is a caveat on the wills. Therefore you would have had to treat with me to remove this obstacle. But did you? No. Your pathological hatred of me (God knows why) with your infantile greed, envy, and selfishness—a toxic combination—prevented you.
>
> Likewise, for these contemptible reasons you could not stand the thought that our parents wished to leave their estates in *equal shares to us both* as stated in their wills of 2000, and your original offer of £25,000 is less than half of what by rights is due to me.
>
> Nonetheless, when negotiations for a settlement were nearing a conclusion, the prospect of giving me even this amount proved unbearable to you, so you thought of a reason to scotch the deal: you have falsely claimed that I

am withholding some of father's diaries in spite of it being repeatedly pointed out to you that this is not the case. It is clear, therefore, that you have negotiated in bad faith.

You know, and you know that I know you know, that you bullied and pressured our parents when they were enfeebled by old age to change their wills to exclude me and leave everything to you. In your desperation to do this you even got Malik Tara to 'witness' father's 2005 will when he was not present with the other signatories; he later swore an affidavit attesting to this fact.

Not only that but you regularly extorted money from our parents amounting to tens of thousands of pounds, to say nothing of Toby's school fees of £39,000 between 1999 and 2001 paid by father that you were too miserly to pay yourself. You had already seized the bulk of father's diaries (even before he died!—which you had no right to do) and although I had managed to keep a few of them out of your clutches, you were not satisfied; you wanted to grab *everything*. (You behaved in the same way when Auntie Eleanor died; her body was hardly cold before you rushed around to her house unlawfully to remove as much of her property as you could.) Now, ten years after our parents' deaths you are still obsessed to get your hands on 'all' of father's diaries and some items of furniture which have long been disposed of—and even mother's plants![22]

When you were a little boy it was a standing joke that you always piled your plate up with so much food you were unable to eat it all. What a pity mother and father could never say 'No' to you!

Furthermore—I have already told you but I'll say it again—although you repeatedly denied knowledge of my private papers and certain of my books, they suddenly turned up at your flat. In other words, your previous denials that you had these items were lies. What were you doing with them

---

[22] In one email he demanded to know what had become of the houseplants at No 81!

anyway? The answer is that you stole them, as you did my portrait. It is clear, therefore, that in addition to the financial and other abuses you perpetrated on our parents and me, you are a liar and a thief.

This is all of a piece with your reputation for unpredictable and violent behaviour. Two women of your former acquaintance with whom I have spoken have admitted they are afraid of you and one of even described you as 'vicious'. Because of this, it is a great pity that an opportunity of putting on another of father's plays has been lost.

Finally, I wish to point out that although the path to our estrangement started from when you sent me a gratuitously offensive email in 2005, even after that and everything else you did or neglected to do, if there had been *one word* of apology or regret from you—a miracle!—our relationship might not have come to this.

A reply came immediately (2 November 2017):

Your toxic and highly nasty correspondence keeps coming decade on decade. You have kept our parents from what you call a decent burial because you have put a caveat on the will entirely unjustly because you didn't want to acknowledge their wishes. You write utter tosh saying that I abused them during their lifetime. I don't know on what basis you say this. They loved me and I behaved as a proper son to them, and looked after them when they were old. What did you do, nothing except create a horrible atmosphere when they were dying because I was in your flat at their behest and finally again attacked me in the hospital….You put me on the street 30 years ago from a flat that our father had meant for me to live there as well that that was his wish and you ejected me… Thus you illegally threw me out when that flat was meant for me as well.

I have tended the grave put down plants and made it as tidy as I could but according to the law I am not permitted to make anything permanent. So again you are talking nonsense when you say I neglected the grave. What have you done; you never even go there, never put flowers. I frequently visit the grave. You once left a miserable cheap bunch of flowers not even taken out of their wrapping, and you call that caring. I never extorted money from our parents. Our mother was afraid that you would bully her as she knew you had always been a bully and you forbade me to visit your flat even when you were in Tokyo. She entrusted the money to Clive with instructions to let me have any as and when I needed it and this he did to keep it out of your clutches. So I did not bully her. She wanted to help me out of her own free will. Clive will testify this under oath if necessary. So most of the money was given to me to help me before she died and was not stolen from her. You can't seem to get it into your thick skull that our parents did things out of their own free will and just because you think you should have had what I had you can't accept this. This is just purely rivalry on your part. You never got over that I was born...I did not seize the bulk of father's diaries before he died he asked me to remove them for safe keeping until your daughter removed about 12 of them. She seized them under your authority. He wanted me to publish them and he knew they were in danger from your history of seizing things and having locks changed.

   I have your rotten books and I never denied having them I have put on father's plays before and intend to do so with others.

   I repeat, as you steadfastly refuse to acknowledge what I say. I did not take anything from the flat other than all the plays which belonged to me. It was a joint venture between me and father. You illegally—yes it was against the law—and I mistakenly thought you would store them until probate was given removed the entire contents of the flat and never informed me. Your pathetic arguments about sending a fax and telling me about storage are just lies. Neither Clive nor I received a fax from you and in any case this must always been backed up by a letter for it to have any veracity...I was never at any stage given the opportunity to have anything from that flat. As I have said before anything I have I was given by them including the portrait which is mine legally and is not stolen as you assert. All the items I am willing to share with you on signing the agreement. You have disposed of everything in their flat a lifetime's history with no possibility for the grandchildren let alone us to have their history. It really is monstrous what you did with their belongings selling a Jung letter written to father for a song and selling off mother's library for nothing, which meant so much to her. I have no chance to have anything in their flat. You won't come clean about any of their possessions. What happened to the Windsor chair for instance? All you can say it was disposed of—that is laughable. I repeat an entire lifetimes' history of both our parents you have just trashed; it is simply terrible.

I will sign the agreement but first I want to know direct from Erica what she did with those diaries and for you to say she finds me vicious is no argument.[23] No matter how she finds me that is no excuse; she could write you and email and you could forward it to me or even send it direct. So get her to say what she did with those diaries at the door; it is that simple and don't fob me off any more prevarications. If you want the agreement signed then do that. You should want to know where these most important years have gone and don't keep telling me she doesn't know. All I am asking her is to say what she did with them. Do you get it?

Then I want to retain all the copyrights including the *Isle of Cats* and mother's book on the midlife crisis you illegally removed from Belsize Lane.

---

23 Tommy is confused about this and much else. I had already told him that Vicki removed these diaries at my request and sent them to my solicitor for safe-keeping. (Subsequently they were sent to me in Japan.) The person who called him 'vicious' was a former girlfriend; my daughter had described him as 'rude and intimidating' and she had nothing to do with removing the diaries.

I have no objection to you looking through any of the diaries I have.

Re your accusations about Auntie Eleanor: yes I took her collection of children's toys farm animals which were worth nothing but the entire contents was removed for which we got nothing anyway so your remarks are ridiculous. Owing to your behaviour we were not given the opportunity to sell anything in her house and this was also down to your hatred of me. As long as I didn't get anything you were prepared for the whole house to be trashed, and history repeated itself twenty years later on the death of our parents. Come clean and tell me what you did with the contents and don't tell me you disposed of it because that means nothing.

Tommy was just getting into his stride; another email came two days later:

You say I abused and bullied the parents without saying how, other than I got them to change their will. Your behaviour takes the biscuit…although mother begged you to come to father's funeral you didn't and you neither came to Mum's and then to add insult to injury you had your own fake funeral in which as a sermon you abused me and moreover said I had caused father's death by not allowing him to come home just because he wanted to. He would have died sooner if I had done that. There were no facilities for him to be looked after in the poisonous atmosphere of 'your flat'…If the parents helped to pay for Toby's fees which was only for a term or two then there is no harm in that. Some parents unlike you, help their children…

The ball is firmly in your court re the signing of the agreement. I hope once this agreement is signed we can be friends again, for the sake of the parents.

These are examples of how Tommy twists and distorts everything and attacks me for situations he himself caused.

Mother didn't beg me to come to the funeral; as mentioned above it was Tommy who gave me just three days' notice to travel from Japan for this event—an obvious impossibility. Father indeed might have died sooner in the comfort of his own home: that was the plan, agreed with by his GP. But Tommy wanted to hold onto him as long as possible for his own needs. The reason there were no facilities for father to be looked after at home was because Tommy refused to make the necessary arrangements—easy enough if you contact a private nursing agency with your chequebook handy. Father didn't pay for Toby's school fees only for a term or two: he paid for nearly three years according to his bank statements which I have. Finally, it's interesting that Tommy adds the comment about being friends again with me. I wonder who told him to put that in. I also wonder how he found out about father's Memorial Service. It was no secret, and I had anyway thought of sending him a copy of the order of service and my speech.

The 'Jung letter' deserves some comment. Since I wished to sell my flat after our parents died I needed to have it cleared. As detailed earlier, Tommy had already removed several van loads including almost everything of value. I did take some of the volumes of mother's Collected Works of C. G. Jung. She had the whole set but about a quarter of the twenty volumes I already had in my library in Tokyo. Therefore I only took only those volumes, with their copious interesting underlinings made by our parents—they both studied Jung—which I did not then possess. Unknown to me, apparently there was an original letter from Jung that it seems was kept in one of these volumes. It is reproduced in *C. G. Jung Letters*, Vol II, 1951–1961, Routledge & Kegan Paul (1976), p 131:

To John Symonds [Original in English] 13 October 1953

Dear Sir,
 The quotation [Charles Lamb, "Witches and Other Night Fears," *The Essays of Elia* (1821)] you have kindly sent me

is indeed very interesting. Thank you very much for it. I know a case in my own experience where children who have been brought up in a too rationalistic way, that is have been deprived of a proper knowledge of the fairy world, have invented fairy tales all by themselves, obviously to fill the gap left by the stupid prejudices of adults.

I know the book about *The Great Beast* [John Symonds, *The Great Beast: The Life of Aleister Crowley* (1951)]. It is indeed beastly beyond words, and very good reading for people who have too optimistic a view of man. Thanking you,

Yours sincerely, C. G. Jung

It is a pity that father did not have this letter framed and put on his wall! Obviously, if it had come into my hands I would have treasured it. Somehow Tommy got to know that it was (presumably) interleaved in one of those volumes which I had arranged to be cleared by a second-hand book dealer in Hampstead. In yet another example of how he misinterprets and twists such incidents to attack me, he accused me of having 'trashed' the entire contents of my flat where our parents lived, which contents he claimed belonged to him!

In the meantime, since Routledge had turned down *Midlife* it stuck in my craw that if I signed the amended agreement I would merely get back my stolen property and he would get everything else. Rather than run up further legal bills I wrote to him directly (7 December 2017):

My solicitor wrote to you on 30 May 2017 in a final appeal to settle this dispute after there had already been long delays on your side. We heard nothing. As a last resort I attempted the unrewarding exercise of direct communication. All this achieved was yet more demands for information that I do not have about the whereabouts of some of father's allegedly missing diaries and you saying that you did not now even want to give me the copyrights of *The Isle of Cats* and *Midlife*!

It is unfair and unreasonable that you withdrew your original offer of £25,000 on the pretext of the non-production of certain allegedly missing diaries. I am unable to assist you with enquiries as to their whereabouts and I believe you are mistaken to think they exist or existed.

Since you have so long delayed responding to our repeated appeals to settle this matter, I wish to inform you that I am now only prepared to settle according to the terms of the original Agreement including your payment to me of £25,000.

Hearing nothing in reply, I tried again on 26 December 2017:

The present state of the correspondence between us is wholly unsatisfactory with a number of matters unresolved.

I'll deal first with one that seems greatly to exercise you: the disposal of certain items belonging to our parents. These include the Jung letter, some photos, and miscellaneous items that turned up in Keith Fowkes's second-hand bookshop Obviously, this happened by mistake and not from any want of respect on my part. I was not present when my flat was cleared and in dealing with a lifetime's accumulated property it was almost inevitable that some items were unintentionally disposed of. Secondly, you complain that you have not received 'your share' of the contents of my flat at No 81. It seems I must remind you yet again that almost all the contents thereof were my property. On the other hand, you removed and presumably still have most of our parents' personal property as previously mentioned. [List appended, as on page 119.]

You make no comment on my refutation of your claim that mother 'gave' you the portrait. It was never her property to give away, as you allege she did. Did she commission and pay for the portrait? No, I did, and I have the receipt from the artist that you can see in the attachment. You are well aware that you unlawfully removed my portrait in or around 2006 for reasons best known to yourself. So let's have no more bullshit about that.

Now let me get to the main point. I don't know if you have read all (or any) of father's novels, children's books, biographies, etc., but I have. They are very well written, highly original, often witty, and hold the reader's attention; they deserve to be republished. I have in recent years received enquiries from various publishers wishing to do this; if we come to an agreement, I'll pass these on to you. But as you know, there's an impediment to republishing our parents' works: the caveat on the wills. Why did I put a caveat on the wills? I've said it before and I'll say it again: you know, and you know that I know you know, that you exerted undue influence to get mother and father to change their wills of 2000 to leave everything to you and nothing to me. There was no reason they would have done this other than your pressuring them. This is unfair and unacceptable.

So we are at a deadlock. I am sure this must be as unsatisfactory to you as it is to me.

Considering that you have contrived to acquire all of our parents' cash assets, and, if the caveats were lifted, would acquire in addition all of father's diaries in my possession, and the rights to their published and unpublished works (with the two exceptions mentioned in the Agreement), even if you gave me the relatively small sum of £25,000, it is clear that you would have the lion's share.

Again, I ask you to reinstate the money and sign the Agreement as it was otherwise last amended.

Finding himself backed into a corner, Tommy stubbornly stuck to his views and refused to answer any of my points. It would be tedious to show all the subsequent correspondence, but even trying to appeal to his better nature to cooperate with me so we could at least get some of our father's works republished, was unavailing.

At one stage Burnet involved himself by writing directly to me. To this, I replied to Tommy as follows (4 November 2018):

> The reason I went through lawyers when faced in 2014 with your shameful neglect of our parents' grave, was to avoid the unpleasantness of direct communication with you. Nonetheless, now that we have been in email contact on a number of occasions, it is simpler that we continue in this way if we have anything more to say to each other.
>
> As I wrote to you personally three days ago, I did not expect to receive a reply on your behalf from that dirty dog Clive Burnett who colluded with you to cheat me out of my inheritance, in which he insolently rejects my latest proposal. You can tell him that any further emails from him will be blocked and will not be read.
>
> You may also care to point out to Burnett that four years ago when I made a complaint about him of professional misconduct to the Association of Certified Chartered Accounts (ACCA), the reason they did not proceed was not because the complaint had no merit, but merely because it was out of time.

I added a postscript to this message:

> Every time you look at the portrait that you stole from me, you will see in our mother's eyes her condemnation of your criminal behaviour!

The letter of complaint that I sent to the ACCA in part was as follows:

> In summary, my complaints against Mr Burnett fall under the following headings of the 2009 version of the ACCA Rulebook:
>
> He may have been in breach of Section 3.4, paras 183 (a) and (b) in that there was a conflict of interest in him being

involved with rewriting John's will in May 2005, since at that time he was acting as a family friend and I was one of his paying clients. In my view, the duty of confidentiality to John, as Mr Burnett claimed, was invalid since under these circumstances he had a duty to inform me that there was a potential conflict of interest or at least had a duty to withdraw from assisting John to rewrite his will. Further, I believe it was not John's true intention to rewrite his will but he was unduly influenced by Thomas with Mr Burnett's involvement and collusion. Thus, he may also have been breach of Section 3.2, paras 5, 11, 12 (c), 13 and 14.

In regard to Mr Burnett assuming control of Renata's cash savings, he may have been in breach of Section 3.20, para 1, and in regard to his refusal to account to me about these savings, as someone who had a legitimate reason to ask, he may also have been in breach of Section 3.20, para 2(c), and that unless he arranged for these monies to be kept in a separate bank account he may in addition have been in breach of Section 3.20, para 10.

A selection from the subsequent correspondence follows:

From me to Tommy, 12 April 2019:

> I should like to have this matter cleared up once and for all. It shouldn't take you too long to consider what I have proposed.
>
> We are both old men now and it would be a great shame for this dispute to remain unresolved and left for the next generation to deal with.
>
> I cannot sign the old Agreement [with no monetary consideration], and for you to demand that I do so as a pre-condition for returning my property is blackmail. This is illegal.
>
> May I ask you to put aside your old resentments and settle this matter in a spirit of compromise? It is pointless to argue

about the contents of No 81 while you have got most of our parents' goods of any value and all their cash!

I shall amend the Agreement and related documents about copyrights to reflect recent changes we have discussed, in particular: that you will put the cash back on the table (let's call it £24,000, being a token reduction in compensation for your disappointment in not getting 'all' the diaries).

Please indicate your willingness to accept these terms. I shall then send you the amended agreement.

Tommy to me, 26 May 2019:

You are barmy. I never stole any of your belongings. They were only contained in boxes together with my things which came into my possession over the years.[24] You are welcome to get them back together with other books that you don't even know about. A pity you chose to dispose of, quoting your very words, the entire contents of No 81 which you malevolently say all belonged to you as if the parents moved into your flat in about 1998 with nothing. I suppose that the Windsor chair and all their clothes etc. belonged to you. At least all the items which are yours, you are welcome to have which I still have, having disposed of nothing. You will not as I have told you many times get £25,000 out of me. Sign the agreement you drew up or there is no agreement. Also for your information I have never offered you £25,000 as you erroneously state.

My last communication with Tommy was sent on 28 May 2019:

The return of my property was part of an agreement proposed nearly five years ago. Unfortunately, you scuppered this agreement by withdrawing your initial offer of £25,000

---

24 This is nonsensical. Does Tommy mean he acquired my belongings by mistake?

for the spurious reason of the non-production of certain of father's diaries which as far as I am aware never existed.

Now you say 'I have never offered you £25K.' Have you gone soft in the head? You made this offer in December 2014 as you can see from the attached copy. There have also been numerous references to it in earlier drafts of the agreement and related correspondence.

Although I was at once stage prepared to accept the original agreement without any monetary consideration, as I have mentioned several times I am no longer prepared to do so. If you are unwilling to put some money back on the table, then we shall indeed have no agreement, as you are so fond of repeating.

An agreement by which this dispute will finally be resolved so that the caveats will be withdrawn thus allowing a proper memorial to be emplaced and for you to gain title to the copyrights of the bulk of our parents' intellectual property, etc., is one thing. It is an entirely different matter that you admit you have somehow got your hands on various property belonging to me which I wish to have returned. You must, therefore, return these items to me to me immediately without preconditions and you have a legal obligation to do so.

This letter was ignored. I have, therefore, regretfully been obliged to let the matter rest.

12

SUMMARY AND CONCLUSION

IN THE COURSE of writing this narrative I formed the hope that I might gain some understanding of Tommy's behaviour. Could a formal psychiatric diagnosis explain it? The one that comes to mind is the so-called narcissistic personality disorder[25] of which he showed several features: a sense of entitlement; selfishly taking advantage of others to achieve his own ends; lack of empathy; enviousness; and showing arrogant, vindictive, and contemptuous behaviour. Psychiatric diagnoses, however, being of necessity entirely subjective, are of limited usefulness.

Nonetheless there certainly *was* something wrong with Tommy, and to deal with this a narrative-based or descriptive approach, as I have attempted in this book, seems best.

As set out in Chapter 2, two factors were strikingly evident: the over-protectiveness shown to Tommy in his childhood especially by our father; and the over-indulgence with which mother and father always treated him. I have often wondered if the rudeness he frequently exhibited to them was a kind of 'cry for help'. If children grow up without proper boundaries, they may, through bad behaviour, unconsciously be pushing their parents in order to seek reassurance that there *are* boundaries. Unfortunately, our parents showed no consistency in 'drawing the line'. Tommy had learnt that if he persisted in his demands, particularly for money, they would usually give in to him. In my own experience of this, such as when I told him I was unable to give a prognosis as to how long some of his physical symptoms would last, instead of just accepting it he repeatedly demanded to know 'Why not?', trying to *insist* that

---

[25] American Psychiatric Association. Diagnostic and Statistical Manual of Mental Disorders, Fifth Edition (DSM-5), American Psychiatric Association, Arlington, 2013.

I told him what he wanted to hear. And if one didn't comply, he often would become angry and rude. As our father said, 'he drives you potty, he goes on and on.' This stubbornness seems to have been a defence mechanism he could not overcome; to have done so would have meant facing himself—not an easy thing to do. Maybe the symbolic meaning of his pains, as father pointed out, was that he needed to deal with something painful within himself; inability to do so will inevitably result in neurosis. This would perhaps explain the impression Tommy created on someone I know who met him in late middle age who described him as 'a very unhappy and embittered person.' A photo of him taken in 2012 (Plate 17) does seem to show these characteristics.

In addition, there was the long-standing emotional dependency he showed towards both our parents. It is a mystery to me why he could not have developed beyond this and stand on his own feet. He also seemed to be stuck in an attitude that allowed of no compromise in disputes: it was always the other person who was wrong—never him.

Where have we ended up? Tommy has estranged himself from his own brother and schemed to disinherit me. He grabbed all our parents' savings and caused them to die in misery. He stole the portrait of our mother that I commissioned as a keepsake, and has attempted to blackmail me with it. And our parents' grave remains without a headstone.

Unfortunately, there seems little chance of the situation improving.

Printed in Great Britain
by Amazon